JACKSONVILLE
AFTER THE FIRE
1901–1919

Merry Christmas, Dixie
& George from Liz &
Don. 1991

Note page 94.

James B. Crooks

University of North Florida Press/Jacksonville

JACKSONVILLE
after the Fire, 1901–1919

A NEW SOUTH CITY

Printed in the U.S.A. on acid-free paper ♾
The University of North Florida Press is a member of the University Presses of Florida, the scholarly publishing agency of the State University System of Florida. Books are selected for publication by faculty editorial committees at each of Florida's nine public universities: Florida A & M University (Tallahassee), Florida Atlantic University (Boca Raton), Florida International University (Miami), Florida State University (Tallahassee), University of Central Florida (Orlando), University of Florida (Gainesville), University of North Florida (Jacksonville), University of South Florida (Tampa), and University of West Florida (Pensacola).

Orders for books published by all member presses should be addressed to University Presses of Florida, 15 Northwest 15th Street, Gainesville, FL 32611.

Library of Congress
Cataloging-in-Publication Data

Crooks, James B.
Jacksonville after the fire, 1901–1919 /
James B. Crooks.
p. cm.
Includes bibliographical references and index.
ISBN 0-8130-1067-5
1. Jacksonville (Fla.)—History.
2. Jacksonville (Fla.)—Economic conditions.
I. Title.
F319.J1C76 1991 91-91
975.9′12—dc20 CIP

Skylines of Jacksonville. Reprinted from T. Frederick Davis, *History of Jacksonville, Florida, and Vicinity, 1513 to 1924* (St. Augustine: Florida Historical Society, 1925), 244.

CONTENTS

ILLUSTRATIONS

ACKNOWLEDGMENTS

Though scholars often work alone in their research or writing, they are rarely independent. Many people help them from the germination of an idea to its completion as scholarship, and my experience is no exception. In the beginning, back in 1982, one of my students, Pat Kenney, was a catalyst when she suggested I should stop talking and start doing research in Jacksonville history.

Libraries and librarians are one's greatest resource. At the University of North Florida's Carpenter Library, people who have helped include Kathy Cohen, Bruce Latimer, Eileen Brady, Peggy Pruett, Mary Davis, and Sandra Creighton. In the P. K. Yonge Library at the University of Florida, Elizabeth Alexander and Steve Kerber assisted me in my research. Carol Harris in the Florida Room of Jacksonville's Haydon Burns Library repeatedly amazed me with both his knowledge of local history and his detective work ferreting out information I could not find. There were also the many unnamed librarians who helped at Edward Waters College, Florida State University, Florida State Archives, National Archives, and Yale University.

The University of North Florida provided assistance with a sabbatical leave in 1984–85 and a research travel grant in 1984 through the Training and Service Institute. The university's Division of Instructional Communications drafted the map of Jacksonville and reproduced eight pictures. The Florida State Archives supplied two photographs, and Judy Davis, a professional photographer, copied the rest. Also of major help at the University of North Florida were support staff, particularly departmental secretaries Deborah Martin, Jacqui Wheeler, Patricia Berry, and Marianne Delegal.

History journals played an important role, too. Samuel Proctor, editor of the *Florida Historical Quarterly*, published earlier versions of chapters

2 and 3. The *Journal of Regional Culture* published an earlier version of chapter 5.

Colleagues in history read, commented, and added helpful insights at various stages. On earlier articles, David Colburn, Raymond Mohl, Jerrell Shofner, and Dale Clifford provided criticism. More recently, David Courtwright and Dan Schafer read the entire manuscript, offering useful commentary. In addition, Morteza Ebneshahrashoob from UNF's Department of Mathematical Sciences graciously advised me on my charts and sampling procedures in chapter 2. Richard Bizot and the UNF Publications Board have provided continuing encouragement. I am grateful to these colleagues for their assistance. Any errors of fact or interpretation, however, are my responsibility.

Finally, my greatest support came from my wife, Laura, whose love, friendship, support, and patience over the years have been a continuing encouragement. To her, I dedicate this book.

INTRODUCTION

When the Atlanta *Constitution* editor Henry W. Grady addressed the New England Society of New York on December 21, 1886, on behalf of regional reconciliation, he also brought to national attention a vision of the New South. The Old South of secession and slavery was dead, he said. Hard-working plain people now "sowed towns and cities" and "put business above politics." In Atlanta, "we have raised a brave and beautiful city. . . . We have planted the schoolhouse . . . and made it free to white and black. . . . We have fallen in love with work . . . [and] have established thrift in city and county."[1]

In the generation after the Civil War, Grady's Old South gentlemen Cavaliers had become industrious New Southerners subscribing to the Puritan work ethic, "uplifting and upbuilding" the region. Grady never pointed directly to the modernization model of the northern states, but his vision paralleled that of the antebellum Yankees sowing the seeds of literacy, hard work, thrift, and uplift across the settlement of the old Northwest.[2]

As for the freedmen of the South, Grady said good riddance to slavery. He praised "this sincere and simple people" who deserved the "fullest protection of the laws." In the New South, they would have the vote and, he added, "our friendship." Further progress, however, would depend

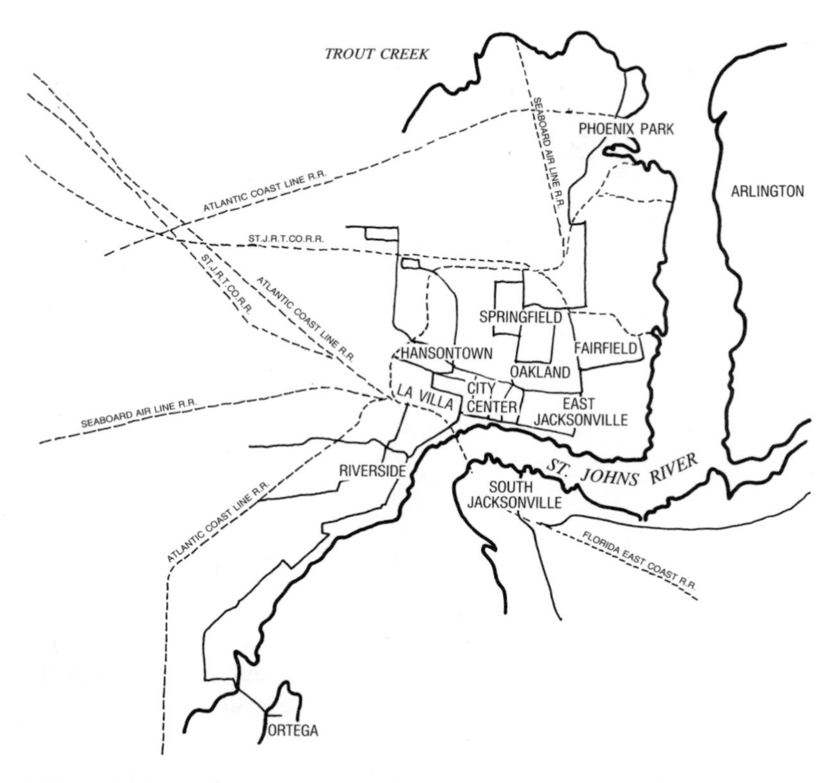

Jacksonville and Vicinity, 1913. Prepared by the Division of Instructional Communications, University of North Florida.

upon "those among whom his [*sic*] lot is cast," namely benevolent white southerners.[3]

Racial paternalism aside, Grady expressed in this New South vision what became a major myth in the history of the region. Journalists, educators, businessmen, clergy, politicians, and even historians became its advocates. They spoke of a new "spirit of enterprise," of a "progressive spirit" prompting "social and industrial change," the abolition of illiteracy, and the development of manufacturing. At its heart was a commitment to economic development, peaceful race relations, and reconciliation between the South and North.[4]

The vision of the New South, of course, never became the dominant reality for the region in the late nineteenth or early twentieth centuries. The South remained predominantly rural, lacking in investment capital, and locked into the destructive systems of crop lien and Jim Crow. Yet islands of development did appear in cities, reinforcing both the vision and the myth. Atlanta best epitomized the New South city because of its rapid reconstruction after the Civil War, its railroad links, its pursuit of northern capital, and Henry Grady. But Atlanta was not alone. Birmingham sprang into existence in the 1880s as a major regional coal, iron, and steel manufacturing center. Nashville, Houston, Louisville, and Richmond became rail centers, and, toward the end of the century, Jacksonville began to develop as a New South city.[5]

Historians writing about southern cities in the late nineteenth and early twentieth centuries tend to stress their backwardness compared with northern cities. Memphis, for example, was portrayed as the murder capital of the nation in the 1880s. The great proportion of every southern city's streets were unpaved, having ankle-deep mud or stifling in dust, depending on the season. Devastating epidemics were frequent. Black city dwellers were particularly impoverished, segregated and victimized by white supremacist businessmen and politicians. Unfortunately, at times all of these portrayals were true.[6]

Yet to compare southern cities then with their northern counterparts overlooks their substantially greater post–Civil War poverty as well as the racism that hampered development. Playing catch-up in an era when northern cities not only had a head start but were developing rapidly was virtually impossible. Effective southern competition with national cities had to await the infusion of federal funds and northern capital in the mid-twentieth century.

Another way of looking at development in the New South city in those years is to compare change over time within the city. According to the myth, this change began at the end of Reconstruction and continued well into the twentieth century. Its first generation was particularly crude in character, having minimal street paving, water and sewer services, law and order, or other urban amenities. The driving force of urban boosterism fostered economic growth. Beginning in the 1890s the second generation saw the development of what historian Don Doyle calls the modern city, with municipal waterworks, electric power plants, urban transportation systems, paved streets, public schools, parks, and other urban attractions.[7]

One need not be a mouthpiece for the Chamber of Commerce to look at these changes in a city's population, economy, physical shape, institutions, popular culture, race relations, and quality of life. Anyone can ask questions. Did the economy grow and diversify? What was the changing character of the city's peoples? What happened to its downtown and residential areas? In what ways did race relations change? Did the quality of life improve, particularly in the areas of health care, housing, education, and entertainment?

Underlying these questions are assumptions about urban life, the New South myth, and American values at the turn of the twentieth century. Did the spirit of enterprise and the work ethic of which Grady spoke take hold in southern cities? Did people develop positive attitudes toward change? Did city building include investment in human capital? How did urban blacks respond to the politics and policies of white supremacy? To what extent did public policy shape urban growth, perhaps at the expense of traditional individual rights? Southern cities were at the heart of the New South myth, and to the extent that they developed new forms, values and life-styles, they brought modernization to the region.[8]

This study examines the rise of one New South city in this second stage of development, after the Great Fire of 1901 destroyed most of downtown Jacksonville. Jacksonville, of course, did not change from a winter resort to a modern city overnight. The seeds of modernization clearly were sown prior to the fire, by the coming of the railroads after the Civil War, the creation of a Board of Trade in 1884, and the introduction of progressive city government by Mayor Duncan U. Fletcher in 1893. The fire temporarily broke the momentum, but rebuilding the city served to stimulate new growth, which in turn brought newcomers to Jacksonville seeking jobs and opportunity. They came from the Florida countryside, from south Georgia, and from as far away as New York, Michigan, and Kansas. These new residents stimulated still further growth.

The character of that growth was shaped by both public policy and private decisions. City, state, and federal governments all played a role in determining the shape of the new city. Private institutions, including the Board of Trade (which later became the Chamber of Commerce), Jacksonville Woman's Club, and black churches, also helped to determine that character. By the eve of World War I, Jacksonville had become a New South city.

By Henry Grady's criteria, the three major goals for the New South vision were fulfilled. Jacksonville's economy had expanded substantially through the port, railroads, banking, construction, and wholesale and retail trade. The city had established racial policies largely satisfactory to the dominant white minority, if not to the African-American majority. There was national reconciliation between this southern city, which had been invaded four times during the Civil War, and the North. Federal troops trained in Jacksonville during the Spanish-American War. President Theodore Roosevelt visited the city in 1905, and northern businessmen repeatedly invested in further economic growth.

Yet in the four decades following Grady's New York address, the vision had expanded. It included J. L. M. Curry's strong commitment to public education as the "cornerstone" of the New South. Curry, southern agent for the Peabody-Slater fund, was a leading advocate for public education, encouraging increased local and state governmental support. In the Progressive Era, from the 1890s to World War I, public policy fostered many New South changes, particularly in the areas of public education and public health.[9]

Meanwhile the physical shape of the New South cities changed. When Jacksonville rebuilt after the fire, new skyscrapers, churches, department stores, a city hall, a public library, and movie theaters created an image of a modern city. An electric streetcar system linked downtown to the expanding suburbs for both the working and middle classes. Growing neighborhoods, both black and white, petitioned City Hall for their own parks, schools, and other amenities, reflecting a civic vitality not always expressed at the polls. Often these expressions came from private voluntary groups, such as the business-oriented Board of Trade, the white middle-class Woman's Club, residential neighborhood associations, or black and white activist churches. Clearly this New South city developed a civic activism that contributed to the vitality of urban life.

Another expression of the New South city could be seen in the use of leisure time. While emphasizing the work ethic in business and labor, local businessmen also encouraged new consumer forms of recreation in amusement parks, movie theaters, ballparks, and department stores (forerunners of today's shopping malls). Local newspapers fostered this consumer consciousness with increased advertising as well as special features on sports, entertainment, and fashion.

In sum, the New South city built upon Grady's vision, changing its physical shape, expanding governmental powers, vitalizing citizen and special-interest groups, and offering a range of activities that frequently competed with traditional values of home, church, and family. In many ways, these changes were playing catch-up with the changes taking place in northern cities during these years. The northern model represented the ideal, as Atlanta became "the Chicago of the South" and Jacksonville's Dixieland Amusement Park "the Coney Island of the South."

There was also a downside to the New South city. Foremost were deteriorating race relations, ranging from expanded segregation laws to disfranchisement and lynchings. The racial harmony of which Grady spoke in New York became the subjugation of black southerners forced into a Jim Crow system. Poverty was another downside in the growing slums of the New South cities. It had, of course, existed before this time, and as long as southern agriculture remained impoverished, refugees from the countryside moved to cities looking for work. Yet as the cities prospered in one area, urban poverty also grew. These extremes of poverty and wealth remained northern problems as well.

A third limitation reflected the dependence of New South cities on social and economic forces beyond their control. The beginning of World War I and the British blockade cut off the export of nitrates, naval stores, and lumber to Germany, resulting in depressed economic conditions in Jacksonville. American entry into the war, however, stimulated the economy with shipbuilding and the establishment of an army quartermaster training camp. In a few short months, Jacksonville's surplus of available housing became a severe shortage.

The war also brought pressure to prohibit the sale of alcoholic beverages. Strong drink met a mixed reception in New South cities. Both traditionalists and progressives advocated temperance. On the one side, temperance went hand in hand with the work ethic, thrift, and the dominant religious institutions of the region. On the other, city boosters recruiting new businesses did not want to convey a spirit of provincialism that might be compared unfavorably with the more cosmopolitan ways of Boston, New York, or Baltimore. Eventually most New South cities banned strong drink. Jacksonville did, too, after the War Department threatened to remove the training camp if it refused.

Historian George Tindall has written about "The Emergence of the New South" occurring between 1913 and 1945. For Jacksonville and other New South cities, a strong case can be made for their emergence before World War I. During these earlier years, southern cities provided leadership for the region just as American cities provided national leadership in economic development, governmental policies, culture, and communications.

ONE

Before the Fire

How do we look at an American southern city like Jacksonville, Florida? Do we see it from today's perspective of a downtown with skyscrapers towering over city sidewalks? Does it include crowded expressways, suburban sprawl, golden arches, and mammoth shopping malls? Is a city primarily known by its headlines or by statistics on poverty and crime? Obviously there are many ways of seeing a city, all of them incomplete. A city is like a kaleidoscope with many patterns and images. To attempt a complete picture is to seek the impossible. Yet we strive, trying to capture a sense of the city and hoping others will accept it.

The New South city, such as Jacksonville between 1900 and 1920, is even more difficult to understand. On the eve of the Great Fire, Jacksonville had many images. Visually, according to maps and photographs, the St. Johns River dominated the city along its southern boundary, flowing northward from downstate, turning east in front of downtown, then north again, and finally to the Atlantic Ocean twenty-two miles away. Along the waterfront, lumber mills, wharves, warehouses, and railroad tracks greeted the waterborne visitor.[1]

The Jacksonville of 1900 spread outward from its city center on the river to the affluent suburb of Riverside to the southwest, prosperous Springfield to the north, black Oakland to the northeast, and white, working-class East Jacksonville and Fairfield eastward along the river.

Residents from the fringe could reach downtown readily by streetcars that ran into the city from all of the suburbs. In town, residents could walk to work, shop, worship, or play. Horsedrawn cabs were also available. There were no skyscrapers. The most majestic buildings were the resort hotels, churches, and handsome homes of prosperous citizens. Boardinghouses for both single people and families accommodated a community that had not yet discovered the apartment house. While housing was generally segregated by race, a surprising number of blacks and whites lived in integrated neighborhoods. A slum named Hansontown housed a substantial number of black residents on the northwest fringe of downtown. Visitors, however, usually saw only the more attractive parts of Jacksonville and considered it a prosperous, progressive city.[2]

This image of a prosperous, progressive city had been developing for a generation in travel books written by contemporary visitors. Poet Sidney Lanier went to Jacksonville in early 1875. He described a community of 12,000 to 14,000 people, which increased substantially in numbers during the tourist season. Much of the economy was geared to tourism. Trains and ships brought travelers to Jacksonville; the major hotels opened only from January to April; shops along Bay Street sold souvenirs of alligator teeth (made into whistles or watches), heron plumes, mangrove walking canes, coquina figures, or palmetto hats for ladies. There were sailboats to rent and excursions available upriver to Green Cove Springs or Palatka. Livery stables leased saddle horses, buggies, and carriages. For more sedentary visitors, a circulating library and reading room provided books and magazines. A conservatory of music offered concerts periodically. On Sundays and weekdays, churches held religious services. For Lanier, tourism far overshadowed the lumber industry. The city was "the main gateway" to Florida.[3]

A decade later publicist James Esgate wrote of the broad streets in downtown Jacksonville, shaded by large live oaks with hanging Spanish moss. He praised the grandeur of the St. James Hotel, capable of housing 500 guests. It occupied a full city block north of a park later named for Confederate veteran Thomas C. Hemming. Esgate also described city growth in the earliest stages of what was to become the New South city. He noted the expansion of the Jacksonville business district north of Bay Street and the early development in the neighboring suburbs of LaVilla, Riverside, Springfield, East Jacksonville, and Fairfield, then beyond the city limits. Commerce, he wrote, played an increasing part in the city's economy with coastal shipping, railroads, wholesale houses, and retail shops. Lumber mills dominated the city's limited industrial base; cigar

Hon. Duncan U. Fletcher, mayor of Jacksonville, 1893–95 and 1901–3. Courtesy of the Haydon Burns Library.

manufacturing ran a distant second. Four banks, including William Barnett's new Bank of Jacksonville, served the community. The most prominent newspaper was the recently merged *Florida Times-Union*.[4]

Jacksonville also had certain modern amenities by 1885, including a telephone exchange. Electricity lighted the St. James Hotel, Park Theater, and shops along Bay Street. Other important additions to the city over the preceding ten years included a public high school for whites, a synagogue, St. Luke's Hospital, a library, a new courthouse, and a Board of Trade. For Esgate, Jacksonville in the mid-1880s was a bustling, growing New South city.[5]

This image of Jacksonville continued despite the depression of the 1890s. Writing in mid-decade, S. Paul Brown described Jacksonville as a center "of finance, commerce and transportation . . . the most important orange market in the world" and a good winter resort. It had expanded its land area to seven and one-half square miles, annexing the neighboring villages of LaVilla and Fairfield. Its riverfront extended nine miles along the St. Johns. Under the new charter of 1893, Mayor Duncan U. Fletcher had begun a wide range of public improvements, including street paving, a municipal power plant, a new City Hall, and enlarged public parks.

Main Street had become a handsome boulevard extending north through Springfield. Reforms in the police, fire, and sanitation departments led to what Brown called "substantial municipal growth unprecedented in the city's history despite the 'hard times' of the past two years."[6]

The private sector supported the municipal efforts. The Board of Trade (later to become the Chamber of Commerce) provided essential leadership in many areas. Its members drafted the new charter, which introduced the Australian secret ballot to local voters. Following the construction of the jetties at the mouth of the St. Johns River by army engineers, the board persuaded the Duval County commissioners to issue bonds to deepen the river channel to eighteen feet. The board sponsored legislation for a state railroad commission to reduce rates for Jacksonville shippers, supported a paid fire department, recruited new businesses including the Clyde Steamship Line to provide regular service to Charleston and New York, supported the construction of the Union Passenger Station, and worked for the electrification of the street railway system.[7]

New and developing urban institutions also drew Brown's attention. By 1895 Jacksonville's private schools included Edward Waters College, Florida Baptist Academy, and Cookman Institute for African-American students, plus St. Joseph's Academy, Massey's Business College, and the Southern Conservatory of Music for whites. Brown noted the absence of any college or university for whites in Jacksonville. He also mentioned the Daniel Memorial Orphanage and Home, the Frankie Schumacher Relief Association Hospital (eventually to become St. Vincent's Hospital), the Colored Orphan and Industrial Home Association, Boylan Industrial Home, St. Mary's Home for Orphan Children, Hebrew Benevolent Society, B'nai Brith, Odd Fellows, Knights of Pythias, Red Men, Masons, Seminole Club, Florida Yacht Club, temperance societies, and militia companies. These voluntary associations involved blacks and whites, Catholics, Protestants, and Jews in Jacksonville on a racially segregated basis.

The images drawn by these three writers over a twenty-year period were largely positive. They showed Jacksonville growing from a small, predominantly resort community in the 1870s to a regional commercial center before 1900. A rich variety of social institutions reflected the beginnings of a modern New South city.[8]

The leading local newspaper, the *Florida Times-Union and Citizen*, provided further evidence of the developing modern city. It reported a banner year in 1900 for the local economy because of increased numbers of ships entering and leaving the port, new construction, and a busy tourist sea-

Main Street Boulevard, Springfield. Courtesy of the Haydon Burns Library.

son. The *TU&C* also gave a sense of the city's cultural vitality, reporting memorable performances at the Park Theater by James O'Neill and Otis Skinner, the minor league baseball season, visits to the Ostrich Farm, summer excursions to Pablo Beach, parades, and festivals.[9]

Jacksonville's rail connections brought prominent visitors to the city. In February 1900 future Socialist party presidential candidate Eugene V. Debs addressed a racially mixed, outdoor audience of 2,500 people at the corner of Market and Forsyth streets. The newspaper described him as a witty and powerful speaker, attacking the rich and championing the poor. Two weeks later William Jennings Bryan spoke to almost 6,000 people at Hemming Park. One listener, a retired Baptist minister and Confederate veteran, later described it in his diary as "the best political speech I ever heard." In March Admiral George Dewey, the hero of Manila Bay, arrived. Thousands greeted and cheered him at the railroad station and on parade to the Windsor Hotel. In December America's most famous mayor, Samuel "Golden Rule" Jones of Toledo, visited Jacksonville after a conference in Charleston. He liked what he saw, commenting on the city's cleanliness and on the municipal ownership of the waterworks and electrical utility. A strong labor advocate, Jones advised city officials to institute an eight-hour day.[10]

Organized labor welcomed Jones in its efforts to play a substantial role in Jacksonville at the turn of the century. The Central Labor Union, comprising sixteen black and white unions, claimed 1,300 members. However, the work force in 1900 numbered more than 12,500, and the unions' major visibility appeared to be its sponsorship of the Labor Day parade.[11]

Still, parades and holidays were important to Jacksonville. On the Fourth of July the railroads scheduled extra trains to carry excursionists to the beaches. The Labor Day parade drew thousands of participants. The greatest celebration, however, was Gala Week, beginning November 26. Every day saw parades of police and firefighters, militia, shriners, marching bands, decorated floats, even babies and the city's five automobiles. There was a golf tournament at the country club, a circus performing opposite the railroad station, horseracing in Springfield, street shows, trapeze performances, and a Thanksgiving football match between the Jacksonville Light Infantry and a team from Macon, Georgia. Merchant Leopold Furchgott called the week "the biggest time ever in Jacksonville with thousands of people from all over the state attending."[12]

For many residents, Thanksgiving meant attending church services in the morning, perhaps browsing afterward in the local shops that were open, and then heading home to sumptuous dinners. Black churches held special congregational Thanksgiving dinners while other caring people prepared special meals at the Confederate Veterans Home and for inmates at the prison farm. A month later residents celebrated Christmas without the commercialism of the later twentieth century. Families came together again to attend church services and then feast on turkey and seafood.[13]

Obviously, in 1900 Jacksonville was not all full stomachs and festivals. A malaria epidemic from August through October caused substantial pain and sorrow, reflected in the increased mortality rates for the year. Fevers were a special scourge in warm weather. The 1888 yellow fever epidemic killed 429 people, and there was a typhoid epidemic among the troops stationed in Jacksonville during the Spanish-American War. Despite local protests to the contrary, city residents in 1900 enjoyed less than optimum health conditions.[14]

Another area of concern in Jacksonville were the schools. One of the South's leading educators, J. L. M. Curry of the Peabody/Slater Fund, came to the city in March hoping to find the local schools, he said, "as progressive as the rest of your city." He was disappointed. There was not one schoolhouse he visited "from which plaster had not fallen from the wall or ceiling." Teachers were uncertified and inadequately paid. The school year was less than six months, leaving, he said, "school children with half a year of idleness . . . to forget that which was taught them during the all too short term."[15]

The state superintendent of public instruction agreed. His biennial report in 1900 described the low priority and underfunding of education in Florida. Duval County was no exception. It had the state's largest school system and spent the most money, but per-pupil expenditure of $12.08 per white child and $5.47 per black child ranked it only seventh and eleventh, respectively, among the other counties within the state. The county enrolled 6,765 children (51 percent white) in segregated schools, but average daily attendance totaled only about two-thirds that number. There was no compulsory school attendance law. The school year lasted only 101 days in 1899–1900, or less than five months, compared with a national average of 143 days, or seven months. Northern schools by contrast stayed open for nine months. Of Duval's 169 teachers, six (including one black teacher) had degrees from a college or normal school. Of 131 teachers taking the state certification exam in 1900, only 72 percent passed. Salaries varied by race and gender, with white males on the average receiving the most, white females second, and black males third. Black women earned less than $40 per month for a five-month term compared with street cleaners who earned $30 monthly twelve times a year.[16]

Salary discrimination against black teachers was not atypical of life in the community in 1900. Despite comprising 57 percent of Jacksonville's 28,429 residents, the local 16,236 African-Americans lived in a city where whites held disproportionate wealth and power. Most blacks lived in poverty on the fringes of downtown; a large number inhabited the Hansontown slum. Most adults did menial work with little opportunity for advancement. Schools, hospitals, hotels, restaurants, theaters, churches, trains, and steamboats generally were segregated. A poll tax limited political activity.[17]

Yet if Jacksonville's blacks saw a policy of white supremacy characterizing their city, they also saw themselves struggling to advance within their own community. Since Emancipation, many blacks had worked hard to fulfill their vision of the American dream. Their leaders urged them to practice frugality, thrift, self-reliance, and moral improvement. They encouraged education, voting, and the work ethic. By 1900 a small black middle class had emerged in Jacksonville. It included 49 ministers, 69 teachers, six doctors, three lawyers, one pharmacist, and 131 businesses, mostly small, operated by men and women—barbershops, restaurants, retail groceries, laundries, shoe repair, and dressmaking establishments. In the building trades, skilled carpenters, masons, and bricklayers belonged to local unions. More affluent blacks built substantial homes in the Oakland and LaVilla sections of the city. Black youngsters attended seven public elementary schools. There were no public high schools open to them in 1900, but four private academies—Edward Waters College, Cookman Institute, Florida Baptist Academy, and Boyland Industrial School—provided secondary schooling for a limited number of older blacks. Jacksonville blacks attended one Presbyterian, twenty-three Methodist, and twenty-five Baptist churches in 1900. They belonged to thirteen black masonic societies, eight Knights of Pythias lodges, and several mutual aid associations, including the Daughters of Gethsemane, Daughters of Israel, and Bethel Aid Society. Music, sports, literary groups, and theatrical presentations also attracted black participation.[18]

Community leaders included James Weldon Johnson in education, Joseph Blodgett in construction, the Reverend J. Milton Waldron at Bethel Baptist Institutional Church, Joseph E. Lee in politics, and Eartha M. M. White in social service. Thus, despite racial prejudice and separate but unequal facilities, many Jacksonville blacks worked hard, worshipped regularly, educated their young, and enjoyed social activities within their community.

Jacksonville women slightly outnumbered men among both blacks and whites. One-third of all adult women worked, and they comprised 31 percent of the 12,589 working people in the city. Most women (76 percent) worked in domestic or personal service, such as laundresses, servants, nurses, or waitresses, and they were predominantly black. More than 300 women worked as dressmakers, 170 women taught school, another 130 worked as bookkeepers, clerks, secretaries, or telephone operators, and 60 worked as sales clerks. There were five women "clergy" (probably nuns teaching at St. Joseph's Academy), one journalist, three physicians, and no lawyers. Jacksonville's work force generally was structured like a pyramid with a small business and professional class at the top expanding to a broader base of skilled, semiskilled, and unskilled workers at the bottom. For women, as for blacks, the pyramid was very broad at the base with few people employed near the top.[19]

Women, of course, could not vote, but they had organized into sororities and clubs. Most prominent was the Jacksonville Woman's Club, formed in 1896. In addition to bringing Curry to Jacksonville in 1900, it had raised $600 to keep the schools open when the county Board of Public Instruction ran short of funds. It also endorsed "progressive" candidates in the school board elections. Women comprised the governing board of St. Luke's Hospital, and during Gala Week they dressed in nurses' uniforms and solicited financial contributions from the revelers. The hospital, unfortunately, was continually on the brink of insolvency, reflecting

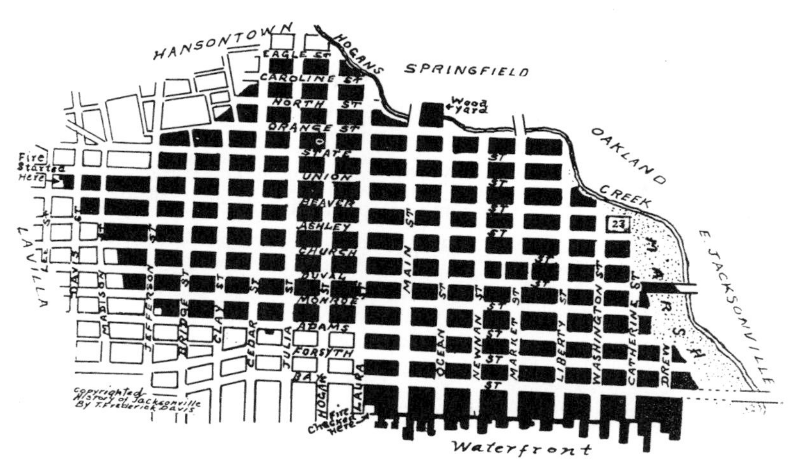

Map of area burned in the fire of May 3, 1901. Reprinted from Davis, *History of Jacksonville*, 325.

in part its managers' economic powerlessness. Women had also founded the first library for whites in 1877, though by 1900 control had passed into the hands of male trustees. Finally, women provided cultural leadership in the recently organized Friday Musicale. Thus, within their limited realm, Jacksonville's women, both black and white, were expanding their boundaries in 1900.[20]

At the turn of the century, Jacksonville was Florida's major metropolis. Its 28,429 residents far outnumbered the 17,747 people living in Pensacola, 17,114 in Key West, 15,839 in Tampa, 2,841 in Orlando, or 1,681 in recently incorporated Miami. Yet seen from the perspective of other southeastern cities, Jacksonville seemed small. Not only Atlanta and Birmingham exceeded it in population; so did Savannah, Charleston, Augusta, Montgomery, and Mobile. Nationally, Florida's first city ranked only 142d in population. By regional and national standards, Jacksonville was insignificant in size. Its immigrant population was also small, numbering only 1,166 foreign-born residents, or 4 percent of the population. Like most southern cities (Tampa and New Orleans excepted), Jacksonville did not attract large numbers of immigrants, in part because of limited industrial opportunities combined with the job competition and low wages paid to blacks working in the sawmills.[21]

What can we conclude from these multiple images describing turn-of-the-century Jacksonville? Each has a portion of the truth, and yet there remains more. None of the sources discussed the political scene in any significant way. Newspaper readers learned that Jacksonvillians voted for Bryan over McKinley in the presidential election, but not that most blacks were effectively disfranchised. They knew that the state Democratic Convention met in Jacksonville and that Floridians had elected William S. Jennings governor, but they saw little mention of Jacksonville's colorful mayor, James E. T. Bowden, or members of the city council. The historical Jacksonville of 1900 then is but a glimpse of the complex, vital, diverse city at the end of the nineteenth century.[22]

□ The new century began hopefully. The Florida tourist season opened in January with sixty-three trains entering and departing from the city. An estimated 15,000 visitors spent that entire winter in town. Henry Flagler's Continental Hotel was under construction at Atlantic Beach and scheduled to open in June. Martha Waldron, wife of the minister at Jacksonville's largest black church, proposed an industrial school and home for African-American boys and girls at Bethel Baptist Church, modeled after Hampton Institute. Nearby, the trustees of Edward Waters College discussed moving away from Jacksonville in order to establish industrial and agricultural departments. Booker T. Washington's ideas for self-help clearly were popular. Meanwhile the Central Labor Union helped organize a state Federation of Labor to improve conditions for working people of Florida. In March the St. Luke's Hospital trustees raised $2,000 with a fair, and the Woman's Club managed to keep Duval High School open for the full spring term.[23]

The Jacksonville fire began on Friday, May 3, 1901. At about 12:30 P.M., sparks from a woodstove fire, drawn up a chimney, ignited Spanish moss drying on outdoor platforms next to the Cleveland Fibre Factory at the corner of West Beaver and Davis streets in LaVilla. Workers on lunch break discovered flames and tried to extinguish them with buckets of water. A brisk northwesterly wind arose, however, and the factory, "a dry pitch pine building with a shingle roof," caught fire. By then the fire department had joined the fight, but its efforts were in vain. When the factory roof collapsed, burning particles spread to neighboring buildings. Within minutes wooden shanties in nearby Hansontown were ablaze. More wind and the fire became "an ocean of flames" half a mile wide roaring eastward, devouring everything in its path, including handsome frame houses, the Windsor and St. James hotels, seventeen churches and synagogues, schools, clubs, office blocks, City Hall, police and fire stations, the armory, and the courthouse. One reporter subsequently wrote,

The Jacksonville fire. Reprinted from Caroline Rawls, comp., *The Jacksonville Story* (Jacksonville: Jacksonville's Fifty Years of Progress Association, 1950), 18.

"the burning of a hotel like the Windsor would ordinarily be regarded as a disaster in itself, but yesterday it lapsed into relative insignificance."[24]

One newspaper reporter attempted to describe the scene: "When the fire reached Julia Street, it was a roaring furnace, without any prospect of being put under control. . . . So fierce was the blaze and so strong had become the wind that millions of sparks and flying burning shingles spread over five or six blocks, setting the roofs of the houses on fire. . . . They burned like cigar boxes, like chaff, as the thundering, mighty, lurid, storm-wave of fire rolled to the east . . . and swept the area bare."[25]

At Hogan's Creek, the fire shifted to the south and blazed its way to the river. Observers feared it would next double back along Bay Street and the waterfront, but about 7:30 P.M., the wind died and the fire department finally gained control.

The next day a reporter looking east from Bridge (now Broad) Street saw "a desert of gaunt ruins. . . . From Bridge to Laura Street, a thin finger three blocks deep stands uninjured along the river front, but to the eastward . . . an unbroken bed of ashes meets the eye in which giant chimneys rear themselves like monuments in some forgotten city's cemetery." The fire consumed 455 acres on 148 blocks, two miles long and nearly a mile wide. A total of 2,368 buildings, including 1,700 homes, were destroyed. The homes or businesses of 9,500 people were destroyed. Estimated property losses totaled $12 to $15 million, with insurance covering about $5 million. Five whites and two blacks died in the fire. Jacksonville faced the crisis of a generation, not unlike the Chicago fire, the Galveston hurricane and tidal wave, or the subsequent catastrophes in Baltimore and San Francisco.[26]

TWO

After the Fire: Economic Growth and Development

Americans from near and far responded to Jacksonville's crisis. Suburban residents opened their homes to friends and acquaintances. Cots were set up in schools and churches until army tents arrived by train from Virginia. Railroads, steamships, and express companies cooperated to rush provisions to Jacksonville free of charge. In Baltimore, *The Herald* began preparing a relief train. The mayor of Charleston, South Carolina, sent a check for $1,000. Folks in towns and cities across the country raised funds for assistance eventually totaling almost $225,000.[1]

The response of the New York State Chamber of Commerce and Merchants' Association of New York City stood out. They organized a special Jacksonville Relief Commission, which shipped $55,000 worth of food, clothes, bedding, hoes, shovels, and wheelbarrows, and 127 portable toilets. William Mills, Jr., a staff member of the Merchants' Association, went to help in its distribution. His subsequent report praised the "herculean efforts" of the people of Jacksonville in responding to the devastation.[2]

That Saturday morning, the day after the fire, Florida Governor William S. Jennings declared Jacksonville under martial law, assigning local and out-of-town militia to guard duty at the entrances to the still-smoldering burned district. All restaurants and saloons were closed. Mayor J. E. T. Bowden met with city council members, the Board of Public Works, and the Board of Bond Trustees. They agreed to send a delegation to a mass meeting called earlier by the Board of Trade, to devise plans for the relief of the destitute.[3]

The mass meeting resulted in pledges of $15,000 for relief and the organization of the Jacksonville Relief Association. Its fifteen-member executive committee represented the community's leadership. It included Charles E. Garner, president of the Board of Trade as chair; Mayor Bowden; Joseph R. Parrott, vice-president of the Florida East Coast Railroad; Episcopal Bishop Edwin G. Weed; Municipal Court Judge Morris A. Dzialynski; Father (later Roman Catholic Bishop) William J. Kenny; bank president and state legislator Dr. J. C. L'Engle; insurance broker (and later developer) Telfair Stockton; railroad executive and lumber manufacturer Wellington W. Cummer; attorney Augustus W. Cockrell from the Municipal Board of Bond Trustees; banker Joseph H. Durkee from the Board of Public Works; grain and feed wholesaler William A. Bours; saloonkeeper and city councilman Harry Mason; and saloonkeeper/political activist Conrad Brickwedel. Attorney Joseph E. Lee, who also was Collector of Internal Revenue, represented the black community.[4]

Seven subcommittees were formed to look after finances, distribution of food and clothing, temporary housing, sanitation, transportation, jobs, and the identification of the people who had lived in the burned district. Subsequently, a special Woman's Relief Committee was appointed under the leadership of Mrs. Catharine Eagan and later Mrs. Nina Cummer. It provided special assistance to white women and children. Black community leaders formed a Colored Relief Association, headed first by builder Joseph W. Blodgett and later by attorney J. Douglas Wetmore, to coordinate efforts among their people.[5]

On Sunday, two days after the fire, the Commissary Committee began distributing food and supplies from black and white relief stations to "between 2000 and 3000 people." The Employment Committee began to receive applications from blacks and whites for jobs cleaning debris. The militia opened a Relief Emergency Hospital. By Monday the Lodging Committee had placed 500 cots in suburban schools to accommodate homeless people. That same day the city issued its first building permit for the burned district. Meanwhile, the newspaper printed notices identifying the temporary locations of homeless people. With his rectory burned, Father Kenny from the Church of Immaculate Conception boarded with a family in East Jacksonville. Francis Conroy, manager of Armour & Company and later president of the Board of Trade, had located his family at the Travellers Hotel.[6]

In that first full week after the fire, Jacksonville began to live again.

Workmen cleaned streets and erected tents for local government offices. Trains arrived from the North with supplies. Temporary structures arose to enable Towers Hardware, Rhodes-Futch-Collins Furniture Company, the Atlantic, Valdosta and Western Railway, and other businesses to resume operations. The Woman's Auxiliary established a temporary laundry and sewing tent, putting seamstresses to work. At the Bethel Baptist Institutional Church site, carpenters began erecting a temporary structure for Sunday worship.[7]

Church losses from the fire were heavy. Roman Catholics lost their church building, orphanage, convent, parochial hall, and priests' residence, worth an estimated $150,000. Insurance covered one-third the value. On May 9 the Bishop of St. Augustine appealed to Catholics across the nation for contributions. Methodists and Baptists also appealed for help nationally to rebuild their sanctuaries. Mt. Zion African Methodist Episcopal Church lost not only its sanctuary but also its affiliated Edward Waters College. Ebeneezer Methodist Episcopal Church lost Cookman Institute in addition to its church building. Both were only partially insured, as were the Congregational, Presbyterian, Lutheran, Christian, Christian Science and Jewish houses of worship.[8]

Meanwhile the religious community improvised at their worship services. Baptists and several other congregations initially worshipped under the trees in Riverside Park. Ebeneezer Methodist Church held services at the Boylan Home Chapel, west of the city. At the site of the Church of Immaculate Conception, under tents "rude benches of dressed lumber supported by burnt cans . . . and pieces of masonry were used. The altar of dressed pine boards . . . was covered with white linen altar clothes . . . and the chalices which were saved . . . were on the altar."[9]

By mid-May workmen had cut down all burned trees and telegraph poles, dug up stumps, cut and removed tangled and useless wires, cleared and begun filling the bulkheads along the river, torn down dangerous walls and chimneys, and cleaned and sorted brick. They hauled debris from the armory, city buildings, churches, and school lots. They graded streets and repaired sidewalks. Meanwhile the Sanitation Department worked closely with the city health officer, the superintendent of sewers, and the plumbing inspector. Workers removed dead animals, filled unsanitary wells, repaired broken plumbing and sewers, maintained clean conditions in the temporary camps and hospitals, provided sanitary closets at the camps and in the burned district, applied disinfectants, and removed night soil. The waterfront, where burned wharves exposed decayed wastes, was a major concern. Laborers provided fill to extend bulkheads into the river where wastes and piped sewage could be washed by the currents out to sea. The result was a substantial if temporary improvement of sanitary conditions along the waterfront.[10]

Hemming Park had become a tent city for the Woman's Auxiliary, "pitched on scorched grass, alongside of gaunt skeleton trees." To the dozen or so tents came white women and children in need of assistance. Families received food, clothing, bedding, and kitchen utensils. One tent housed a dispensary. In another, women operated sewing machines making household goods and clothing.[11]

Not all the cleanup went smoothly. At first there were too few picks and shovels available to clear the debris. Later the Sanitation Committee had difficulty finding men to cart night soil. On May 11 the Clyde Steamship Company and the Naval Stores Company complained about the unavailability of workers. The Relief Committee investigated and concluded that many able-bodied men were taking advantage of the commissaries, avoiding work and sending their wives to collect rations. In response, the Commissary Department issued identification cards to heads of families listing all immediate family members. Daily rations then were allocated to applicants only after their cards were initialed or punched. Meanwhile, Joseph E. Lee reported that black refugees were without stoves. Cooking their meals on bricks was difficult. The commissary issued eight stoves for the black camps.[12]

During the early stages of relief and debris removal, only limited thought was given to the shape of a rebuilt Jacksonville. Nationally the idea of planning beautiful cities had received a boost at the 1893 Columbian Exposition in Chicago, but the local impact was marginal. A *Times-Union* editorial envisioned planning a new Jacksonville with a beautiful riverfront, fireproof wharves and office blocks, new government buildings, hotels, tree-lined streets, parks, and handsome residential neighborhoods. In practice, however, the city council had only limited authority. It passed legislation requiring fireproof brick construction downtown and began work on new government buildings. Jacksonville was not unique. Few cities at the turn of the century planned for the growth or development of their communities. For example, following its disastrous fire of 1904, Baltimore undertook no city planning either. Jacksonville's council did authorize the Atlantic, Valdosta and Western Railway to run tracks along Bay Street in return for completing the bulkheading of the riverfront, but that was a decision of questionable value toward beautifying the city.[13]

In June voters elected Duncan U. Fletcher mayor. The forty-two-year-

St. James Building, housing Cohen Brothers Department Store, designed by H.J. Klutho. Courtesy of Robert C. Broward.

old Fletcher represented the progressive spirit of Jacksonville. Born in Sumter County, Georgia, on the eve of the Civil War, he grew up in Monroe County, son of a modestly successful cotton farmer who owned eight slaves and 530 acres. The Civil War disrupted but did not devastate the family economy. Fletcher was able to attend and graduate from the newly founded Vanderbilt University and Law School in 1881, after which he moved to Jacksonville to join a legal partnership with his college roommate, John M. Barrs. Fletcher's law practice expanded with Jacksonville's economic growth in the 1880s. He also wooed and married Anna Louise Paine, daughter of a prominent New York family, who had come south to Jacksonville. She subsequently led Fletcher to become a Unitarian and principal financial supporter for the local congregation.[14]

Meanwhile Fletcher entered public life. He ran successfully for the city council in 1887, the state legislature in 1892, Jacksonville mayor in 1893, and again in 1901. In his first term as mayor, Fletcher initiated a number of public improvements, including construction of a municipal power plant. He also chaired the local school board and library association. Subsequently he became a major power within Florida's Democratic party and was elected to the United States Senate in 1908. He served there until his death in 1936.[15]

Fletcher recognized how badly the fire had hurt Jacksonville. Half the

Jacksonville's new City Hall, designed by H.J. Klutho. Courtesy of the Haydon Burns Library.

taxable property base of the city had been destroyed. Most of the public buildings were gone. Fletcher had lost his own home. In his inaugural address to the city council, the new mayor urged members to avoid factional or partisan controversies. "The one all-absorbing idea now," he said, "is the restoration of Jacksonville."[16]

That summer and fall, both private and public sectors began rebuilding downtown Jacksonville. The newspapers reported banker W. B. Barnett's plans for a new house at First and Main streets, W. W. Cleveland's intention to build a new fiber factory at the old site, and the decision to rebuild the Windsor Hotel. The school board released pictures of a handsome new brick structure, the combined Central Grammar and Duval High School. The new Stanton School for blacks, however, would be a two-story frame structure. New housing, an apartment building, office blocks, and retail shops began to appear. In July the Presbyterians authorized work to begin on their new sanctuary. Father Kenny began work on a new Church of

Henry John Klutho, Jacksonville's premier architect. Courtesy of Robert C. Broward.

The Cummer lumber mill. Courtesy of the Haydon Burns Library.

Immaculate Conception. In September the Reverend E. J. Gregg reported construction underway on a new Mt. Zion AME Church. By the end of the year, a new Congregation Ahavath Chesed had opened its doors at Laura and Union streets.[17]

During that summer Henry John Klutho, an ambitious young architect, arrived in Jacksonville from New York City to make his mark. Born into a substantial, small-town, midwestern, German-American family in 1873, "Jack" Klutho moved to St. Louis at age sixteen to study for a business career. There exposure to building plans for new office construction led him to consider architecture as a career. Klutho moved to New York to study design and practice with local firms. A year in Europe followed by work experience back in New York prepared him for Jacksonville, where over the next generation he would become the city's leading architect.[18]

Klutho's first contract was for the six-story Dyal-Upchurch Building, the tallest structure in the city at the time. He also designed Temple Ahavath Chesed, T. V. Porter's new mansion (home of KBJ Architects in the 1990s), the First Baptist Church, Carnegie Library (a law firm in the 1990s), and the new City Hall (since torn down). Klutho's early work was neo-classical, Gothic, and Romanesque, but very well designed. About mid-decade, however, he began to shift to the radically new "Prairie School" of architecture recently introduced by Frank Lloyd Wright.

Increasingly Klutho's residential designs began to emphasize horizontal lines hugging the earth, while expanding outward in space. In 1910 the Cohen Brothers asked him to design their new department store. The resulting St. James Building facing Hemming Park became what biographer Robert C. Broward called Klutho's "Prairie School Masterpiece."[19]

Also significant for the city were the new houses built in the burned district for Porter, Mayor Fletcher, U.S. Senator James A. Taliaferro, Florida East Coast Railway vice-president Parrott, and others. Suburban development had begun, but in the early twentieth century prominent citizens still chose to live downtown, maintaining an environment that integrated residential and commercial life.

The effort to rebuild in 1901 did not exclude time for play. That summer the Florida East Coast Railroad ran excursion trains to the beaches every weekend. In June the handsome new Continental Hotel, built by the railroad, opened at Atlantic Beach, becoming an attraction for affluent vacationers from Florida, Georgia, Alabama, and the Carolinas. Independence Day fell on a weekend in 1901, and the *Times-Union* estimated that one-quarter of the city's population must have gone to Pablo or Atlantic beaches.[20]

Jacksonville celebrated Labor Day with a parade of 2,000 black and white carpenters, painters, cigar makers, plumbers, longshoremen, barbers, tinners, lathers, railroad yardmen, stevedores, coachmen, and dairymen marching to Hemming Park. Unions had played a major role in local politics in the 1880s. Though weaker since the poll tax disfranchised many black and white workers in 1890, they still made their influence felt in the city's economy.[21]

Local residents had other diversions. Jacksonville's only theater had burned in the fire, but James Burbridge constructed a temporary facility to open the fall season. In September the newspapers reported the return of the ostriches from their summer quarters at Atlantic City. The Ostrich Farm had been Jacksonville's main tourist attraction since its opening in 1898. The city's two amateur football teams representing militia companies, the Jacksonville Rifles and the Jacksonville Light Infantry, began practicing for their schedule against Valdosta, Savannah, Macon, Lake City, Georgia Tech, and South Carolina College. A new Seminole Club, Elks Club, and Florida Yacht Club along with improvements to the Florida Country Club, which had not been burned, were underway.[22]

Six months after the fire, the city hosted the Florida State Fair. Of major interest were tours of the burned district. Already more than half the homes had been rebuilt and one-third of the offices and shops replaced. Visitors missed the stately oaks and the St. James Hotel, but a new Windsor was under construction. When hotel space ran short, many people stayed in local homes. Thanksgiving became a special holiday to celebrate the city's renaissance. In addition to religious services, there were football games, a golf tournament, hunting and fishing parties, a dance at the Yacht Club, and dining extravaganzas at the hotels.[23]

While by the end of the year life was still not back to normal, Jacksonville had recovered from the fire remarkably well. Insurance money helped finance the new construction. City and county governments issued bonds for new public buildings. The resulting economic stimulus helped shape the next decade and a half of prosperity for Jacksonville.

□ The railroads and the port played major roles. The Seaboard Air Line was already in Jacksonville in 1900. Two years later the Atlantic Coast Line completed its takeover of Henry C. Plant's system. Meanwhile New York financier J. P. Morgan bought the Atlantic, Valdosta and Western and took control of the Georgia Southern and Florida Railroad. Across the river, Flagler's Florida East Coast line had already made Jacksonville its northern terminus as it expanded southward to Miami and Key West.[24]

During these years the railroads expanded their facilities in Jacksonville. West of the city the Seaboard built a major complex of shops and yards. Just west of downtown, next to the Union Passenger Terminal, jointly owned by the Seaboard, Florida East Coast, and Atlantic Coast lines, the railroads built warehouses between Bay Street and the river. Morgan's Southern Railway ran tracks along Bay Street between downtown and the docks. To the east along the river were more warehouses. Out Talleyrand Avenue and into northeast Springfield, the Southern established the St. Johns River Terminal Company and built machine shops, more warehouses, and piers down to the water's edge. At one point the *Times-Union* complained that the riverfront had become almost completely owned by the railroads and shipping companies.[25]

The port also expanded, aided by a river channel deepened first to twenty-four and then to thirty feet. Where previously most shipping was coastal in character, trade expanded to the Caribbean and across the Atlantic to Europe. The major products included lumber, naval stores, and fertilizer; citrus exports and oil from Venezuela became increasingly important on the eve of World War I. Passenger ships of the Clyde Line began daily scheduled trips from Jacksonville to Savannah, Charleston, New York, and Boston. The Merchant and Miners Company sailed daily to Baltimore, Philadelphia, and Boston. By 1914 the Chamber of Commerce could claim that Jacksonville competed favorably with the port of Savannah. The construction of municipally owned docks that was underway augured well for the future.[26]

The impact of port and railroad development stimulated the growth of wholesaling and to a lesser extent manufacturing for the region, both characteristics of the New South city. Jacksonville served as a regional distribution center for consumer goods. In 1905 it had 180 establishments wholesaling meats, liquor, groceries, drugs, hardware, dry goods, electrical supplies, and machinery. More than 500 retail shops provided goods and services. One observer claimed the wholesale grocery houses alone exceeded in number those of Charleston, Savannah, and New Orleans, prompting the Board of Trade to boost Jacksonville as the "Gateway to Florida."[27]

Industrial development proceeded more slowly. Most of Jacksonville's manufacturing establishments were small. Exceptions included Wellington Cummer's lumber mill and phosphate plant north of the city, employing 1,150 workers; the Merrill Stevens Company, which had the largest dry dock south of Newport News and the largest shipbuilding and marine facility in the Southeast; and the Wilson and Toomer fertilizer plant, which claimed to be the largest south of Baltimore. More characteristic of new businesses during the era was the opening of branch plants, such as the Cheek-Neal Coffee Company to manufacture its Maxwell House blend, or the Pepsi Cola bottling company in LaVilla.[28]

Other expansion included insurance, banking, and advertising. In 1901 five black Jacksonvillians led by a Baptist minister, J. Milton Waldron, founded the Afro-American Industrial and Benefit Association (forerunner of Afro-American Life Insurance Company), to provide health insurance and death benefits for the black community. Following founder William Barnett's death, the National Bank of Jacksonville became the Barnett Bank and the largest of thirteen in the city. In 1914 Charles Anderson, proprietor of Anderson Fish & Oyster Company on Broad Street, started a bank in the Masonic Temple down the street to encourage black savings and provided capital for black businesses. At about the same time, Jacksonville's first advertising agency began a campaign to sell the city and state to northern tourists, part of a twentieth-century trend.[29]

A promising new direction in economic development began in 1908 with the arrival of the first film production company from wintry New York. Attracted by the sunshine and warmer climate, sandy beaches and lush vegetation, lower land and labor costs, and the initial enthusiastic support of the local citizenry, half a dozen production firms built studios, shot hundreds of films, and introduced stars such as Oliver "Babe" Hardy, a Georgia native, to the silver screen. By 1914 the *Florida Times-Union* claimed "the motion picture business . . . as a most important one in Jacksonville." Florida film historian Richard Alan Nelson has written that "the area attracted so many movie troupes that Jacksonville became known as the 'World's Winter Film Capital.' "[30]

The prosperity of these years before World War I stimulated suburban growth. To the southwest, Riverside expanded outward toward Willowbranch, Avondale, and Ortega. To the west, on both sides of the railroad yards, developers built Murray Hill, Lackawanna, and Grand Park as working-class suburbs for railroad employees. To the northwest, along Kings Road, Joseph Blodgett, among others, constructed new housing for blacks in College Park, Northside Park, and Highland Heights. To the north, Springfield expanded beyond the city line northward toward Panama Park and the Trout River. To the east and northeast, off Talleyrand Avenue near the mills, warehouses, and river, modest houses filled empty lots. Linking all of the suburbs to downtown were the streetcars of the Jacksonville Electric Company. It more than doubled its track mileage over these years. Meanwhile, across the river, South Jacksonville's more than 2,000 residents secured a city charter from the legislature in 1907. Ferry service connected downtown with this suburban city, which was home to a railroad, fertilizer factory, Dixieland Amusement Park, homes, churches, schools, and shops.[31]

In downtown Jacksonville, a skyscraper boom began in 1908 with buildings of ten stories and taller. A Savannah investor financed the Bisbee office building and the Atlantic National Bank on Forsyth Street, both of which still stand in the 1990s. So, too, do the old Florida Life Insurance Building and the Rhodes-Futch-Collins building. In all, some half a dozen structures changed Jacksonville's skyline dramatically. At ground level, a new City Hall, Carnegie Library, Cohen Brothers department store, YMCA, hotels, churches, and streets congested with autos, trucks, and streetcars gave the city a modern look. Progress, however, could also mean destruction. The handsome palm trees on Main Street extending into Springfield were cut and the grassy median paved in 1916 to facilitate commercial traffic.[32]

While early twentieth-century business statistics may seem small in comparison with later years, a few examples can indicate the size of the growth in Jacksonville after the fire. City real estate values more than quadrupled from 1900 to 1914 (from $11 million to $50 million), as did personal property values (from $2 million to $9 million). Port tonnage in-

Jacksonville's skyscraper district. Courtesy of the Haydon Burns Library.

creased from 650,000 to 4 million tons per year, while the dollar value of exports jumped from $269,000 to $1.3 million. Imports increased even more, from $62,000 to $1.5 million, a clear indication of Jacksonville's important role as a distribution center. Daily passenger train arrivals numbered forty-six in 1900 and ninety-one in 1914, while the number of passengers jumped from 3.5 million to 17 million. Bank clearings totaled $12.7 million in 1900 and almost $175 million in 1913, while postal receipts increased from $91,000 to $532,000 in those years. All of these figures indicate a very substantial growth for the Gateway City.[33]

This substantial growth did not come free of conflict, however. In a city where construction became a major industry, construction workers felt underpaid, initiating strikes in 1902 and 1905. In the earlier year, carpenters wanted $2 for an eight-hour day while the builders wanted nine hours of work for the same wage. In July the Central Labor Union called a general strike, and 2,500 men shut down most of the construction industry in the city. The Board of Trade offered to mediate informally, but the Builders Exchange, the contractors' trade association, rejected any form of arbitration. Gradually, however, job pressures mounted and individual contractors began to accept the eight-hour day. By early August three-fifths of the workers were back on the job, having achieved their goal.[34]

The 1905 strike was a different story. Again the carpenters struck, along with brick masons, claiming a 50 percent increase in the cost of living over the preceding five years and asking for a $2.50 starting daily wage. Besides, electricians and plumbers were earning $4 to $8 per day. The Builders Exchange responded by locking out all union workers. Soon 800 to 900 workers walked off their jobs, including plumbers, plasterers, and painters. The builders responded by importing strikebreakers from as far away as Baltimore. When the strikers sought to prevent them from working, the Builders Exchange secured a court injunction. This time the contractors held firm and the workers lost. The builders had strengthened their control over the construction industry.[35]

On October 29, 1912, streetcar workers struck against the Jacksonville Traction Company in response to the firing of several senior employees for organizing a branch of the Amalgamated Street Railways of America. Stone and Webster of Boston, parent to the local company, had a strong anti-union policy and immediately began importing strikebreakers from New York. Violence followed with strikers cutting trolley lines, throwing rocks and bottles at streetcars, and pulling conductors and motormen from platforms. The governor mobilized the militia to restore order and keep the streetcars running. City council leaders questioned the mobilization. Banker John N. C. Stockton saw it as overreacting, and Senator Fletcher agreed. Supporters called a mass meeting to hear union grievances. The Board of Trade offered to mediate, and negotiations led to wage increases but no union recognition. The strike continued with sporadic violence, but the streetcars still ran. On November 12 the Central Trades and Labor Council threatened a general strike. The Traction Company responded by offering to reinstate striking workers. The Labor Council then backed down, leaving the workers little choice but to renounce the union and return to work. Organized labor in Jacksonville had suffered another defeat.[36]

Labor shortages in the sawmills affected the Jacksonville labor scene in mid-1906, but the unions could not take advantage of it. Mostly the demand was for unskilled workers, and the unions organized only skilled labor. City council members discussed passing a vagrancy law to force idle blacks and whites to work when the discovery of a state antivagrancy law prompted calls for its enforcement. On September 2 seven black men were convicted for hanging around a pool hall in LaVilla. Sentenced to jail, they became liable to work as contract labor in the state's notorious turpentine camps.[37]

Another threat to the economy was too-rapid growth. Beginning in 1906, rail congestion at the port blocked exports of lumber as well as imports of goods for wholesale distribution. Further investigation showed

Forsyth Street, Jacksonville. Courtesy of the Haydon Burns Library.

inadequate storage facilities and too few terminals. Commercial growth had exceeded the system's ability to accommodate it. Again the Board of Trade intervened and, working with the State Railroad Commission, persuaded the railroads to expand their rail lines, storage facilities, and terminal space, temporarily eliminating the bottleneck.[38]

The financial panic of 1907 affected economic growth in Jacksonville, but only temporarily. No banks closed, but that fall the sawmills ran on short time, naval stores shipments were down, and in January the Seaboard Air Line went into receivership, laying off 300 workers in the city.[39]

Yet these were minor detours on the road to prosperity. Jacksonville's population more than doubled in the first ten years of the twentieth century, from 28,429 to 57,699. This increase alone suggests that the city was a magnet attracting blacks and whites seeking to improve their living standards. The Chamber of Commerce in 1914 issued a report celebrating the Gateway City as the commercial, financial, transportation, and distribution center for Florida. It continued to be a resort center with its hotels, amusement parks, golf courses, band concerts, theaters, movie houses,

Table 2.1. Job Categories, by Race, 1900–1910

	Blacks		Whites		Total	
	No.	%	No.	%	No.	%
Class I: high white collar						
1900 census sample	4	2	30	27	34	13
1910 census sample	3	2	25	18	28	10
Class II: low white collar						
1900 census sample	5	3	42	38	47	17
1910 census sample	13	9	58	41	71	25
Class III: skilled blue collar						
1900 census sample	28	17	29	26	57	21
1910 census sample	23	16	43	30	66	23
Class IV: semiskilled/service						
1900 census sample	70	43	6	5	76	28
1910 census sample	58	40	14	10	72	25
Class V: unskilled and menial service						
1900 census sample	55	34	3	3	58	21
1910 census sample	38	33	2	1	50	17
(no employment data)			3	2	3	1

SOURCE: 1900 United States census manuscripts, 1 percent sample; 1910 United States census manuscripts, 0.5 percent sample.

river excursions, and beaches. Its residential neighborhoods were new and charming. Its population and trade had exceeded the major coastal competitors of Savannah and Charleston. From the chamber's view, Jacksonville was a city of the New South and destined to lead the growth and development of the entire state over the next few years.[40]

□ If the overall picture of Jacksonville showed substantial growth and prosperity, beneath the surface different conditions existed. While the Chamber of Commerce evaluated the economic growth of the early twentieth century by examining the change in gross figures such as bank clearings, port tonnage, and rail traffic, U.S. census enumerators counted individual Jacksonville residents in 1900 and 1910, recording what sorts of jobs they held, whether they had been unemployed during the previous twelve months, and whether they owned their homes. The census takers also identified residents' states of birth and literacy. All of these characteristics help to show who lived in Jacksonville in 1900 and 1910 as well as changes that took place there between those years.

For research purposes, rather than counting and classifying each individual head of household listed in the manuscript census, I systematically chose, compiled, and compared a 1 percent sample of Jacksonville's population in 1900 and a 0.5 percent sample of its population in 1910. Tables 2-1, 2-2, and 2-3 show another side of the city.[41]

Table 2-1 examines categories of employment by race ranging from high white-collar professional and business people to unskilled and menial service workers.[42]

Several conclusions can be drawn from this sample about economic conditions for Jacksonville residents during this decade of prosperity. First, most white Jacksonvillians in 1900 (65 percent) were classified as white-collar workers. Less than 10 percent of the white population were semiskilled or unskilled workers. In contrast, most black Jacksonvillians (77 percent) were semiskilled or unskilled workers. Only about 5 percent, primarily teachers and clergy, were white collar. On the other hand, a substantial 17 percent of blacks were skilled workers: carpenters, bricklayers, masons, and painters. The dominant image, however, is one of a relatively affluent white Jacksonville and a relatively poor black Jacksonville.

A second conclusion relates to the changes that took place between 1900 and 1910. Most significantly for the community as a whole, the proportion of white-collar residents increased from 30 to 35 percent. This suggests improving economic conditions. So does the influx of skilled workers over the decade, a large number of whom worked for the railroads. For the black community, the increase in white-collar workers reflected the increased number of small black businesses in 1910 employing clerks and salespeople. While many of these small businesses were marginal economic ventures with potentially high failure rates, they also reflected black enterprise seeking greater economic independence and opportunity. For whites, the significant increase was among skilled and semiskilled workers, suggesting a beginning of the "blue collarization" of Jacksonville that has characterized much of the twentieth century. The decline of white business executives and professional people was only proportional, not absolute.

Overall, despite increases in white blue-collar workers and black white-collar workers, the dominant character remained the same in Jacksonville. Fifty-nine percent of white Jacksonville remained white collar and 76 percent of black Jacksonville was semiskilled or unskilled workers at the bottom of the economic ladder. In a city where one-half of the population was black, these figures suggest a major underutilization of black talent, which would hinder subsequent urban growth in the twentieth century. Jacksonville, in effect, was an economic engine running on barely more than half its cylinders.[43]

Table 2.2. Black and White Unemployment, Homeownership, and Literacy in Jacksonville, 1900–1910 (percentages)

	Blacks	Whites	Total
Unemployment for past 12 months			
1900	21	4	16
1910	13	4	9
Homeownership			
1900	24	29	26
1910	14	30	22
Literacy rate			
1900	86	97	91
1910	75	99	87

Table 2-2 compares unemployment, home ownership, and literacy in Jacksonville in 1900 and 1910 for blacks and whites.

Several conclusions can be drawn from table 2-2. First, while unemployment figures were not kept systematically as in the late twentieth century, census data did show individuals who were unemployed at some point in the preceding twelve months, as an indicator of economic conditions. In Jacksonville, this rate of unemployment for blacks declined over the decade from 21 to 13 percent, a sign of real economic progress. Still, according to our sample, blacks in 1910 remained three times as likely to be unemployed as whites.

Second, the proportion of homeownership in Jacksonville in 1900 appears to be low. However, at the beginning of the twentieth century, most residents in cities across the country rented their accommodations. The figures suggest a further decrease from 1900 to 1910, but they are slightly misleading as the actual number of homeowners increased with the increase in population. More significantly, white homeownership increased both proportionately and absolutely, while black homeownership declined. This decline may have resulted from uninsured homes lost during the fire, but it also suggests that with slightly improved economic conditions, blacks still faced economic barriers, probably a shortage of housing and most certainly racial discrimination in the housing market.

Third, the decline in black literacy at a time when the city's black population increased from 16,236 to 29,293 suggests a failure in the segregated public schools of the South. Its effects would add to the greater difficulties blacks had advancing in jobs above the most menial levels.

Table 2-3 shows the state of birth for Jacksonvillians in the sample for 1900 and 1910, by race. "Other South" refers to the states of the Con-

Table 2.3. Place of Birth for Jacksonville Residents, by Race, 1900–1910

	Blacks		Whites		Total	
Place of birth	No.	%	No.	%	No.	%
1900						
Florida	104	63	50	42	154	54
Other South	58	35	27	23	85	30
North	1	–	28	23	29	10
Foreign country	2	1	11	9	13	5
1910						
Florida	45	31	27	19	72	25
Other South	99	69	62	43	161	56
North	–	–	31	22	31	11
Foreign country	1	–	22	15	23	8

federacy other than Florida. "North" refers to the remaining states of the union.

Table 2-3 takes into account the more than doubling of the city's population during these years. The increase came largely as a result of a substantial immigration from nearby southern states. The proportion of Florida-born Jacksonvillians dropped sharply, from one-half to one-quarter of the total, while the number of other southerners almost doubled. With minor variations, such as the substantial increase in the white foreign-born population, this shift occurred for both blacks and whites. By 1910 only one-third of the black population and one-fifth of the white population were native to Florida. The great southward migration of the twentieth century had begun, but for Jacksonville, unlike downstate, it was predominantly southern in character.

By 1910 Georgia-born Jacksonvillians in the sample actually outnumbered Florida-born locals for both blacks and whites, perhaps influencing the later tongue-in-cheek title for the city as "The Capital of South Georgia."

The significance of this migration for Jacksonville is not entirely clear. The incoming blacks did not affect the literacy rate, nor the level of jobs blacks in general held. Black non-Floridians had proportionately the same literacy rate and did as well vocationally as Floridians. What may have changed was more subtle. James Weldon Johnson, black scholar, poet, artist, and statesman, remembered late nineteenth-century Jacksonville "as a good town for Negroes." In contrast, twentieth-century Jacksonville became a "one hundred percent Cracker town," reflecting a greater southern character in race relations. Quite possibly this early twentieth-century in-

Abraham Lincoln Lewis, founder of the Afro-American Life Insurance Company. Courtesy of the Carpenter Library, University of North Florida.

flux of both whites and blacks from nearby southern states contributed substantially to shaping the harsher racial attitudes that developed during these years in Jacksonville.[44]

□ Still another way of looking at economic change for Jacksonville residents during these years is through the city directory. This approach entails matching the names from the 1900 census sample with the city directories of 1900/1901. Two hundred seven people could be identified by name, address, and employment from both sources. Their employment profile approximated the employment profile from the census sample. I then traced these 207 people in the Jacksonville city directory for 1902, 1905, 1910, and 1914.

The results generally confirmed the census samples about employment in Jacksonville. Whites held most of the white-collar jobs; blacks worked mostly at relatively menial tasks. Several other characteristics were also noteworthy.

First, upward mobility was limited among the 87 people traced from 1900 to 1910. Only 11 people (13 percent) of this sample moved up one or more classifications, such as from skilled blue-collar to white-collar employment. This compares with 18 percent in selected northeastern cities and about 20 percent upward mobility in rapidly growing cities, such as Atlanta and Los Angeles. Jacksonville's lack of upward mobility cannot be explained in racial terms, as more blacks in the sample advanced than did whites. Blacks, however, tended to advance from unskilled to semi-skilled jobs whereas whites moved from blue- to white-collar employment. Instead, the stability may suggest that most whites in 1900 (two-thirds) were already well situated, and most blacks (75 percent) were stuck on the lower rungs of the economic ladder. Examples of white mobility included George Ferry, who moved from being a mason in 1900 to building contractor ten years later; and T. K. Hatcher, who tended bar in 1900 and was vice-president of a wholesale grocery firm at the end of the decade. Black mobility was exemplified by Needham Gaston, who was a barber in 1900 and, a decade later, had his own shop with his son working for him; and Elijah Bellamy, who began the century as a livery stablehand and became a carpenter.[45]

Perhaps most successful and clearly atypical of African-American mobility in the sample of blacks was Abraham Lincoln Lewis. Lewis was a mill machinist in 1900. A year later he helped organize the Afro-American Industrial and Benefit Association and became its first manager and treasurer. The Afro-American Insurance Company, which grew out of the association, became a major Jacksonville business. Another success story was August Blum, a German-Jewish immigrant in the 1880s. He began the century as a clerk and by 1910 owned his own wholesale and retail liquor company. Substantial upward mobility, however, was the exception rather than the rule.

More characteristic were people in all classifications who remained in the same job through the years. For example, Philip Prioleau (white), was city engineer in both 1900 and 1910. Columbus Drew (white) practiced medicine. Rosecrana Pollard (white) taught high school. Alexander Johnson (black) worked at a sawmill. Kate Barnes (black) was a laundress. Edwin Heston (white) worked as a telegraph operator. David Capers (black) was a carpenter throughout the decade. This relative lack of upward mobility was not atypical in American cities at this time.[46]

Another significant finding from the city directories was the substantial movement of people spatially over time, as seen in table 2-4.

Of the 207 people identified in both the census sample and the city directories, 60 percent moved the first year, either within the city or away from the city. Doubtless the fire's destruction contributed to this mobility. However, between 1902 and 1905, two-thirds of the remaining people

Table 2.4. Spatial Mobility, 1900–1914 (percentages) (1900: N = 207)

Directory	No change in address	Moved in city	Left city	Returned to city	No data	Total no.
1900–1902	37	30	30	–	3	207
1902–5	33	29	29	8	–	153
1905–10	42	21	28	10	–	120
1910–14	38	18	35	8	–	95

SOURCE: *Jacksonville City Directory*, 1900, 1901, 1902, 1905, 1910, 1914.

surveyed moved into, out of, or within the city. The numbers declined thereafter (as does the representative character of the sample), but clearly for any year examined, less than half the residents remained at the same address.

Over the ten years from 1900, 56 percent of the people sampled left the city; by 1914 59 percent left, a proportion comparable to the numbers leaving Mobile, Omaha, San Francisco, or Boston during this era. Why did so many people leave these cities? Historians Howard P. Chudacoff and Judith E. Smith have suggested that "many people who left one place for another, particularly unskilled workers, . . . were probably moving in response to patterns of layoff and unemployment, exchanging one low-paying job for another. Others, however, did find greener pastures. . . . Thus although cities frustrated the hopes of some, they offered opportunities to others." Jacksonville was no exception.[47]

Over fourteen years in Jacksonville, almost 90 percent of the original 207 people either died or changed their address. Some people moved two and three times. Alexander Johnson (black), Francis Gage (white), Julia Vance (black), Armstrong Steadman (white), Luke Tolliver (black), and Rufus Russell (white) moved at least three times during the first decade of the twentieth century.

The exceptions were folks like attorney Horatio Bisbee (white), who rebuilt his home on West Beaver Street after the fire and stayed there; Andrew Connor (black), who lived above his grocery store on Leila Street through the decade; Charles Garvin (black), living on West Union Street; or Susan Lee (white), minding her boardinghouse on Hubbard Street. But these people really were unique to Jacksonville.

This restlessness characterized not only Jacksonvillians but also the thousands who moved to the Gateway City during these years, more than doubling the local population. The influx was not predominantly of either race. Similar proportions of both blacks and whites immigrated. By socio-economic class, there were distinctions. Skilled workers were most likely to move, perhaps reflecting job opportunities in a decade of prosperity. Lower white-collar people were least likely. The mobility at both the top and bottom of the economic ladder approximated the mobility of the whole group, which was substantial. One wonders to what extent this mobility affected people's loyalty or sense of identification with and belonging to Jacksonville.

What can we conclude from sampling the census and directory materials? First, the economic indicators for the city tell only part of the story. The prosperity of the banks, railroad, shipyards, wholesale houses, and sawmills did not indicate the well-being of a majority of the citizenry. In fact, the people shared very unevenly in Jacksonville's progress.

Overall, there was some progress between 1900 and 1910, as seen in the increased proportion of white-collar and skilled blue-collar workers and the decline in unemployment (tables 2-1 and 2-2). African-Americans, however, participated only to a very limited extent. As a result, Jacksonville remained a city limited in its growth potential, in part due to barriers of racial segregation and prejudice that blocked substantial upward mobility for one-half the population. The Chamber of Commerce at the end of the era presented an image of a prosperous Jacksonville. Behind the affluence of downtown, Riverside, and Springfield, however, lay widespread poverty in Oakland, Hansontown, LaVilla, and Brooklyn. Both were characteristics of New South cities.

□ Another weak foundation of Jacksonville's economy was its dependency on outside forces. Reduce trade and the city's economy suffered. On the eve of World War I, the local economy slumped. The suburbs were overbuilt and downtown construction exceeded demand, idling construction crews and curtailing the real estate market. Under normal circumstances, the economy would have gradually adjusted and resumed growth, but the outbreak of war in August 1914 sharply aggravated the situation. Exports of naval stores and phosphates to Europe virtually ceased—federal authorities considered both commodities contraband or conditional contraband. The dollar value of exports in Jacksonville dropped 76 percent in one year, and stayed down until the United States entered the war in 1917. Lumber exports dropped by one-third. The impact upon the port, sawmills, fertilizer factories, and naval stores industry was substantial. The financial community was also affected: two banks, including one that had just completed a fifteen-story office building, went bankrupt. The Florida Life Insurance Company followed suit.[48]

Next came the almost total collapse of the real estate market and con-

Masonic Temple, home of Anderson, Tucker and Company, bankers, and other black-owned businesses. Courtesy of the Eartha White Collection, University of North Florida.

struction industry. During the summer and fall of 1915, wrote T. Frederick Davis, "It was estimated by rental agents that one-third of the stores, one-half of the . . . houses, and 60 percent of the office space in Jacksonville was vacant." End-of-the-year figures showed local construction down 56 percent. It would not regain momentum until the outbreak of war.[49]

Unemployment became a major problem in an era when no government programs existed to provide a safety net. The city's primary welfare agency, the privately funded Associated Charities, reported in December 1914 that an increased number of homeless people were seeking assistance. Six months later it described the distress and need among white families in Jacksonville. It was the worst in the six-year history of the agency. Relief funds, however, had run short and jobs simply were unavailable.[50]

The *Times-Union* tried to maintain an upbeat tenor about conditions, rarely reporting the hardships. But even it recognized that one-third of the city's property owners had not paid their taxes, in part due to hard times. Eventually the paper acknowledged that the city's economy had suffered three years of stagnation.[51]

More forthright was the secretary of the Board of Trade. In his annual report at the end of 1914, he recognized, with perhaps some exaggeration, "one of the most trying years in the history of our country due to the depression and financial stringency." Mayor J. E. T. Bowden, reelected in May 1915, put it more bluntly. He asked the city council to reduce city wages by 25 percent. Tax receipts were only 41 percent of budget, times were hard and the city had to cut back.[52]

For black Jacksonville, the recession had a push-pull effect. Generally excluded from white philanthropy and victimized by segregation and discrimination, many young African-Americans responded by leaving town. The war had stopped European immigration. Railroads and northern industry needing labor began to recruit black workers in the South. By early 1916 Jacksonville had become a center for Florida blacks migrating north. Over the next four years some 40,000 Floridians, including 6,000 from Jacksonville, left to seek work under what they hoped would be more attractive conditions.[53]

The recession in Jacksonville bottomed in 1915, but its effects continued into the following year. Recovery began in the fall of 1916 and continued with a major expansion of the Merrill-Stevens Company on the eve of the American entry into the war.[54]

□ In conclusion, Jacksonville developed as two cities in the years after the fire, one white and one black. One city was largely prosperous, creating a commercial gateway to Florida by steamship and rail, developing a regional distribution center for the Southeast, and expanding financial services to provide capital for further development statewide. Enterprise was expressed visually in its port, railroads, skyscrapers, department stores, churches, and handsome suburbs. Limitations were seen in the buffeting by national and international economic forces. Yet overall, as seen by the Board of Trade and daily newspapers, this Jacksonville communicated optimism and commitment about building a modern city in the spirit of the Atlanta model for the New South.

The other city contrasted sharply with the prosperous one. Its residents were mostly poor, worked in low-skilled jobs, and lived in crowded slums. They lacked the resources and opportunities of the white city. Still, they tried. African-Americans built churches and homes, a handsome masonic temple, private schools, a hospital, and a life insurance company. They opened a bank, published a weekly newspaper, started businesses, and created community pride. Yet poverty continued to plague the black city. Discrimination blocked access to jobs above a menial level. When hard times came in 1914–15, thousands emigrated to the North.

This picture of two Jacksonvilles corresponds to the descriptions of other New South cities of the era. In Atlanta, Birmingham, Houston, and Nashville, the media reported and praised the substantial white progress while generally ignoring the barriers that thwarted black development. Contemporary African-Americans knew it, but recent voter disfranchisement blocked efforts to shape government policies that might alleviate the extremes of progress and poverty existing on the eve of World War I.

THREE

Public Policy and Urban Growth

Jacksonville's substantial though uneven growth and development during the years between the Great Fire and World War I owed much to local, state, and federal government policies. The starting point was the state, which had ultimate control over its cities. Florida's Constitution of 1885 authorized the state legislature "to establish and abolish municipalities, to provide for their government, to prescribe their jurisdiction and powers, and to alter or amend the same at any time."[1]

At times the legislature acted with vigor. In 1889 it disfranchised all Jacksonville voters and directed the governor to appoint the city council, which in turn chose the mayor. Four years later the legislature returned the franchise to local voters to elect their mayor and council. Then in 1917 the legislature created a five-member city commission with one commissioner performing the ritual duties of mayor. This council-commission form of government lasted until the city was consolidated with Duval County in 1968.[2]

Behind the state's intervention in Jacksonville's affairs lay local political conflicts. A coalition of white Republicans, blacks, and organized labor had gained control of city government in 1887, defeating conservative Democratic incumbents. In the city elections of that year, voters chose a Republican mayor with a labor-dominated city council, including five blacks. African-Americans subsequently served as municipal judge, chaired the board of police commissioners, and filled twenty-three positions on the police force. Following the yellow fever epidemic of 1888, white Jacksonvillians claimed the city had been misgoverned and sought legislative help. The disfranchisement of 1889 returned city government to white control. The passage of a poll tax, also that year, effectively excluding most poor black and white voters, paved the way for the return of the local franchise four years later.[3]

The transformation from a mayor-council form of government to a commission-council form in 1917 was a variation on the shift to city commission in many New South communities. It began gradually and climaxed abruptly. Following Duncan Fletcher's election as mayor in 1893, the city council passed a $1 million bond issue for public improvements, including the construction of a municipally owned electric power plant (the forerunner of the Jacksonville Electric Authority). The council also established a Board of Bond Trustees to oversee the bond issue. It subsequently broadened the bond trustees' authority to include running the power plant, waterworks, and fire department. In 1911 the Florida legislature placed the Board of Public Works and Board of Health under the bond trustees' control. As a result, the state changed Jacksonville from a strong mayor-council system of government to a weak mayor-council, supplemented by a strong, independent, nonelected authority, the Board of Bond Trustees. The *Florida Times-Union* felt uneasy, concluding that the nonelected trustees had too much "controlling power in the city."[4]

The bond trustees were leading citizens of the community, both honest and autocratic in their use of power. Initially appointed by the governor, later choosing their own successors, and eventually selected by the city council, they were substantially removed from the democratic process in an era when reform-minded Americans across the country were "opening the system" with direct primaries, direct election of United States senators, and votes for women. Many local voters wanted the bond trustees elected, too, but could not reach a consensus on how to achieve it.[5]

What to do remained a problem. The Central Civic League, a coalition of neighborhood associations in Jacksonville, proposed the nationally popular Galveston-Des Moines plan for commission-government, where a small number of elected officials formed a single board replacing both the mayor and the council. The city council ignored this recommendation and passed a charter amendment putting the powers of the bond trustees into its own hands. Opponents of this proposal feared such a concentration of power in a city council known for its favoritism and spoils of office, and persuaded voters to reject the charter amendment in a referendum.

In 1915 Mayor Van C. Swearingen called a charter convention including council members, leading citizens, and representatives of neighborhood and civic groups. It drafted a compromise keeping the city council intact but creating an elected commission to replace the mayor and bond trustees. Jacksonville voters, however, rejected this proposal by almost a three-to-one margin. Opponents this time felt the compromise form was too complicated and lacked adequate procedural safeguards. Finally in 1917 the Duval legislative delegation led by House Speaker Ion Farris secured a charter amendment without a referendum handing Jacksonville its council-commission government.[6]

To Farris, the change democratized local government. It gave the voters a voice in the selection of the men who, he hoped, would continue the honest efficient work of the old Board of Bond Trustees. Others were less optimistic. Perhaps more significantly, the reform of local government represented not the will of local voters who had rejected the new charter in the previous year, but rather the community's leadership influencing the state's determination to impose the charter.

The ability to shape and reshape Jacksonville's form of government over the years reflected the state's total power as defined in the constitution. Fortunately, it was used only rarely. In fact, scholars have criticized Florida's government during these years for its generally conservative, laissez-faire role as compared with more progressive states, such as Wisconsin or California. This criticism is not entirely warranted. State action cuts many ways, and during these years the state actively fostered white supremacy. In 1901 the legislature passed the Democratic primary law, which effectively excluded black Republican voters from participating in the selection of candidates on the Democratic ticket in this predominantly Democratic state. Six years later it gerrymandered election districts in Jacksonville to remove black representation from the city council. It also passed Jim Crow laws segregating formerly integrated streetcars and passenger trains. In effect, the state actively reinforced the white supremacy provisions of the 1885 Constitution, which had provided for segregated schools, a poll tax, and a ban on interracial marriage.[7]

Yet the state legislature during these years also acted constructively. It loosened constitutional restrictions on state aid to education, enabling localities to increase taxation in support of public schools. It enabled Jacksonville to authorize bond issues for civic improvements up to 10 percent of its tax base without prior state approval. In 1913 after several attempts, it passed a child labor law limiting the age, hours, and working conditions for youngsters. It also authorized pensions for police and fire-

Jacksonville Terminal Station (subsequently Prime V. Osborne Convention Center), completed in 1919. Courtesy of Wayne W. Wood.

men. One of its most significant acts created a state railroad commission to regulate rates and prevent carrier discrimination against commercial carriers.

First organized in 1887, the Florida Railroad Commission accomplished little. Disbanded and re-created in 1897, it began a systematic effort to limit the excesses of Florida's railroads in the twentieth century. It intervened in the rail congestion that blocked lumber exports and imports of goods for wholesale distribution at Jacksonville's port in 1906–7. The commission concluded the tie-up at the docks was due to "the unwillingness of the railroads to incur the extra expense of additional trains." Following a series of fines by the commission, the railroads began to improve conditions. They enlarged and improved dock and terminal facilities, repaired and strengthened roadbeds, and added new and improved locomotives and cars. These improvements, combined with the recession of 1907, allowed the congestion to be cleared. By the end of the year, a Railroad Commission report concluded, traffic was "running with a degree of promptness not known for years."[9]

In 1913, following petitions from the city council, the Board of Trade, Real Estate Exchange, and Central Labor Council, the commission opened hearings on the need for a new passenger station in Jacksonville.

The Board of Trade claimed the current station was too small and gave a bad impression to passengers arriving in the city. Further, it said, "conditions . . . are deplorable. Waiting rooms, platforms and toilet facilities are in an unclean and unsanitary condition." The city council's Public Service Committee claimed the station, completed in 1897, was "out of date and sadly deficient in . . . those conveniences which the travelling public demands." [10]

The Railroad Commission agreed and ordered the Jacksonville Terminal Company, jointly owned by railroads serving the city, to build a new station. Plans were submitted and approved. The railroads then requested a new hearing to modify the plans. The commission agreed and then ordered the railroads to proceed. The following May, however, the railroads balked and the case went to court.[11]

Meanwhile pressures built in Jacksonville. Mayor J. E. T. Bowden, after resuming office in 1915, lashed out at the condition of the old station. Four million travelers pass through Jacksonville each year, he said, and it is "an eye-sore to every traveller." Early in 1916, however, the Florida Supreme Court found the Railroad Commission lacked statutory authority in the case. But the effect was achieved. The railroads began work on the new terminal, which was delayed by the war and completed in November 1919. While the state's power to mandate the building of the new station was countermanded by the courts, its actions combined with the efforts of groups in Jacksonville eventually resulted in a new facility.[12]

Clearly, state policies helped shaped Jacksonville's urban growth. Legislation fostering white supremacy after 1900 blocked efforts by Jacksonville African-Americans to rectify social and economic disadvantages at the polls. At the same time, it provided for increasing though incomplete home rule with regard to taxing and bonding, enabling the city to undertake public sector development. Meanwhile state regulation of the railroads limited the power of Jacksonville's largest corporations.

Charter changes affecting the nature of Jacksonville's government had a less clear-cut effect. Seen from the perspective of the late twentieth century after the consolidation of Jacksonville with Duval County in 1968, and the replacement of council-commission government by a stronger mayor and council, the Progressive Era efforts now appear naive. Yet at the time, civic leaders were pragmatically trying to reconcile the political dilemma of people wanting greater honesty and efficiency in government as represented by the bond trustees with those wanting greater democracy. Substituting an elected commission for the Board of Bond Trustees seemed to make sense. In fact, the more popular national reform of combining executive and legislative functions into a commission elected at large frequently led to urban business-civic elites consolidating power at the expense of minority, ethnic, or working-class groups. In Jacksonville the maintenance of a separate elected council at least assured white voters continued representation at the ward level.

Perhaps equally significant, the independent authorities of contemporary Consolidated Jacksonville are the modern-day equivalent for the Board of Bond Trustees. The Jacksonville Electric Authority, Jacksonville Transportation Authority, the Jacksonville Port Authority, and others were empowered for much the same reasons as the bond trustees. State and local groups fearing the excesses of factional politics preferred instead to appoint boards to run government-owned businesses. Seen from this perspective, the state chartering of the council-commission government in 1917 reflected greater trust in the democratic process than most voters had either then or later.

□ If the state in its wisdom held ultimate power over the city, local government both developed and oversaw day-to-day policies and innovated to shape this New South city. The Board of Bond Trustees managed the electric power plant, waterworks, fire department, public works, and board of health. In conjunction with the city council, it set policies for urban development. One of the most important areas of oversight was public health.

Public health improvements in Jacksonville became one of the most significant and lasting achievements of the Progressive Era. Nationally, the decades preceding the turn of the century marked exceptional progress in modern medical science. The development of the germ theory by Pasteur, Lister, and Koch in the late nineteenth century led to the beginning of modern bacteriology, microbiology, immunology, and a scientific basis for public health reforms. Across the nation, cities established policies to advance the health of their communities. Jacksonville was no exception.

Locally public health was a serious concern. The recent history of the city included at least four epidemics of yellow fever, smallpox, and typhoid in the two decades preceding 1900. Climate, environment, and sanitation problems contributed to high levels of communicable disease. Fleas, flies, and mosquitoes were a continual harassment as well as carriers of disease. Stagnant ponds, open cesspools, rotting garbage, muddy streets, dead animal carcasses, and irregular private garbage collection services characterized much of turn-of-the-century Jacksonville. Frequent sum-

Hon. Van C. Swearingen, mayor of Jacksonville, 1913–15. Courtesy of the Haydon Burns Library.

mer cloudbursts and flooding only worsened conditions. In 1900 Jacksonville had a combined mortality rate of 28.6 deaths per 1,000 population, with the black mortality rate 50 percent higher. In contrast, the more progressive city of Milwaukee had a death rate of 14 per 1,000, while Boston, New York, Newark, Philadelphia, and Baltimore had death rates of 19 or 20 per 1,000. Nashville, a leader among the New South cities, had a death rate of less than 22 per 1,000.[13]

Efforts to improve health conditions began following the 1901 fire. New brick buildings, expansion of the sewer system with improved drainage, and bulkheads along the river set new environmental standards for the center city. In 1905 news of a yellow fever epidemic spreading eastward from New Orleans to Pensacola prompted a local war on the mosquito. The city council passed enabling legislation and health authorities began to drain all standing waters, mow tall weeds, drain ditches, and pour oil on ponds to destroy breeding grounds. The epidemic did not reach Jacksonville, and the following year the health department renewed its attack.[14]

At the same time, Dr. Francis D. Miller, the city health officer, began a crusade for a clean city. During the summer of 1906, health inspectors crisscrossed the city checking the condition of fruits and vegetables in the markets, meats at the butcher shops, and milk on the delivery wagons. The Board of Health authorized monthly inspections of all restaurants, cafés, and saloons. The following summer sanitary patrolmen also checked livery stables and dairies for general cleanliness. By the end of the decade Jacksonville's mortality rate had decreased 25 percent, from 28.6 to 20.7 per 1,000.[15]

Still, the black mortality rate remained 50 percent higher, and in each year of the decade black deaths in the city exceeded black births. The *Florida Times-Union* acknowledged that most black neighborhoods lacked city water and sewers, but argued that residents could at least keep their homes clean. Overlooked was the correlation between poverty and sickness where people could not afford adequate food, medical care, or even screens on their windows. More important than the lack of sewers were the outhouses, or privies, plagued by flies. City health officials noted that 80 percent of typhoid cases in Jacksonville came from unsewered houses where flies spread the disease from infected human waste. With the white mortality rate dropping from 23.9 to 15.9 per 1,000 between 1900 and 1910, and with white births consistently exceeding white deaths each year, further substantial public health improvements clearly depended on city officials initiating policies to improve conditions in the black community.[16]

Jacksonville began this effort under the leadership of Dr. Charles E. Terry, who was appointed city health officer in 1910. Terry ranks among the leaders of early twentieth-century public health reform. Born in Connecticut, educated at St. Johns College in Annapolis, Maryland, and then at the University of Maryland School of Medicine, he settled in Jacksonville in 1903 and became a leader in the medical community. Before his appointment as city health officer at the age of thirty-two, he served as chief of medicine at St. Luke's, the city's leading hospital, and president of the Duval County Medical Society.[17]

Terry began building on his predecessors' campaign for a clean city in two ways. First he persuaded the city council to pass a new milk ordinance, establish a bacteriology laboratory, and hire a chemist to begin testing the quality of milk, food, and water.[18] Before the ordinance went into effect, according to the city's dairy inspector, "Jacksonville had the well deserved reputation of having about the poorest milk in the country. . . . It was almost a 'trade custom' to add water and condensed milk in varying quantities . . . and some dairymen nearly doubled their milk supply in this way."

Most milk producers cooperated with the new inspections, but a handful stubbornly challenged the new law, claiming "it was their right to dilute the milk." The courts upheld the city's regulatory powers, and the quality of milk began to improve.[19]

Terry's next step was legislation to regulate the city's privies. They numbered more than 8,500, or almost one for every two families. They were ideal disseminators of intestinal diseases by insect carriers. The privies, Terry wrote, "have all been wide open to flies, and even domestic animals, and in no case are more than fifty feet from a kitchen or dining room. . . . Taken in conjunction with the fact that very few of the houses in the city are screened, and that in the warm season windows and doors are kept wide open, [they] seem to fulfill every requirement for fly transmission of intestinal diseases."[20]

Legislation regulating the construction of privies to make them flyproof by screening was enforced, and the incidence of typhoid dropped dramatically. Terry also pushed for expanding the sewer system with more indoor plumbing, but had only limited success. By the end of his tenure, Jacksonville still had almost 6,000 outhouses, mostly in the black community, but at least the disease had substantially subsided.[21]

Milk pasteurization and screening privies comprised only the beginning of Terry's work. He lobbied for and secured a contagious disease pavilion at St. Luke's Hospital, supported the Woman's Club efforts for a camp for indigent tuberculars, worked with the Department of Public Works to improve conditions at the city's festering garbage dumps, began medical inspections of children in the city schools, and helped start an Infant Welfare Society to provide pre- and postnatal care for white mothers and their children. In 1912 Terry initiated the formation of a Colored Health Improvement Association and hired the first black visiting nurse to confront the greater sickness and mortality in Jacksonville's black community.[22]

Of major concern for Terry were infant deaths, especially among blacks. While most white mothers had doctors attending their births, too many black mothers could not afford a physician and turned to granny midwives for help. Unfortunately, most midwives were untrained in anything approaching hygienic care at childbirth. The result was a black infant mortality rate in 1913 twice that of whites.[23]

Terry disliked midwifery. He regarded the practice as superstitious and ignorant. While a certain racial prejudice undoubtedly colored his views, of greater importance was the fact that Terry saw midwifery resulting in stillbirths, infections, and consequent deaths. He ridiculed grated nutmeg and raisins or lard and bacon fat as proper umbilical dressings. In his annual report for 1913, he described other practices:

> The most approved prophylactic for stomatitis [inflammation of the mouth] is the wiping out of the infant's mouth with one of its own soiled napkins. The occurrence of tetanus in the infant is attributed to the fact that, during labor, the mother did not keep her mouth closed, . . . Of almost general belief is the great danger attendant upon bathing the baby or mother, changing the bedding or even sweeping the room within nine days after delivery and if to such imprudence were added the removal of ashes from the stove or fireplace, it is doubtful if even the most gifted midwife could prevent the dire consequences which would surely ensue.[24]

At the same time, Terry also recognized that most blacks could not afford professional medical care and few doctors took on many charity cases. His solution was a law setting standards for midwifery in Jacksonville and provision for free instruction to women seeking to take the certifying examination. The Health Department also supplied obstetrics kits and supervision by the black visiting nurse. The results were impressive. By 1915 twenty-seven midwives were licensed to assist with childbirths (as compared with sixty-four unlicensed midwives two years earlier). A year later Terry reported that births attended by midwives were considered as safe as births attended by physicians.[25]

Terry's final major program placed him among the country's public health pioneers. Early in his tenure as health officer, he became aware of an extensive traffic in habit-forming drugs carried on by certain physicians and pharmacists in Jacksonville. Though prosecuted under state law, violators escaped conviction due to loopholes, and continued their sales. In 1912 Terry secured a city ordinance requiring the prescription of all addictive drugs, with morphine, opium, and cocaine dosages registered at the Health Department. Addicts could also obtain prescriptions from the city health officer or his designee.[26]

Over a three-year period, the records showed an estimated 1,000 addicts living in the city, or 1.5 percent of the population. Two-thirds of the addicts were whites; over half were women. The most prevalent drugs were cocaine, morphine, and laudanum. Slightly more than half the registered addicts attributed their addiction to medical prescriptions, a quarter to dissipation, and a fifth to the influence of friends (which might or might

Dr. Charles E. Terry, city health officer, 1910–16. Reprinted from Webster Merrit, ed., *Hundreth Birthday of the Duval County Medical Society, 1853–1953* (Jacksonville: Duval County Medical Society, 1954), 99.

not be dissipation). Prostitutes comprised 15 percent of the users, though Terry guessed that might be a low estimate.[27]

Later historians have concluded that Jacksonville's rate of opiate addiction was several times that of northern and western cities. This addiction was a regional, not merely a local, problem. David T. Courtwright has described the southern drug problem as its "hidden epidemic." Many ailing whites became addicted, he writes, through pain-killing prescriptions by physicians who could not cure but who sought to comfort their patients. Patent medicines also played a part. For southern blacks (who used primarily cocaine), drug use may have begun with stevedores in New Orleans using cocaine to endure the long hours and heavy work of loading and unloading ships. This use resembled the South American practice of chewing coca leaves to increase energy, avoid drowsiness, and "bear cold, wet, great bodily exertion, and even want of food . . . with apparent ease and impunity." Jacksonville stevedores, who also were black, may have begun sniffing cocaine for similar reasons, sharing it with workers in the sawmills and turpentine camps. Terry also believed that many black women became addicted in "white houses of prostitution."[28]

Terry's approach to registering and maintaining addicts did not reflect his approval of the practice. Rather he first wanted to examine the size and scope of the problem. Then he looked for alternatives to complete prohibition. Such a radical measure, he felt, would cause great suffering unless there were treatment centers, especially as more than half of Jacksonville's victims had acquired their habit "innocently and unknowingly." The passage of the federal Harrison Narcotic Act in 1914 ended Terry's maintenance program. Although the denial of legal prescriptions for addicts did not become national until after World War I, Terry began phasing out the prescriptions for indigent patients with special detoxification treatment at St. Luke's Hospital.[29]

Terry resigned as chief health officer at the end of 1916, moving to New York City where he became health editor for the *Delineator*, a family magazine. In his final report to the Jacksonville Board of Health, he reflected upon conditions in Jacksonville and his work over the preceding seven years. While substantial progress had been made in reducing the city's mortality rate another 25 percent, from 20.7 to 15.7 per thousand lives, Terry believed Jacksonville's commitment to the public's health still left much to be done.[30]

Of major concern was tuberculosis, the city's deadliest killer, especially among blacks. Neither city nor state had committed to prevention or cure, as had Baltimore and Maryland ten years earlier. For the city's estimated 1,500 cases, there were sixteen hospital beds. Tuberculars prepared and served food in city hotels and restaurants, nursed children, clerked in grocery stores, cut hair, and washed clothes throughout the community.[31]

While tuberculosis remained a major threat, typhoid fever had declined substantially due to the screening of privies. Its eradication awaited the completion of a city sewage system. The city's Public Works department had extended sewer lines into sparsely populated, affluent Riverside, but not into crowded, impoverished, black Hansontown. After seven years, 5,800 privies still served approximately 17,500 persons, roughly one-quarter of the population.[32]

Terry was pleased with the reduction in the infant mortality rate due in large part to the Infant Welfare Society, the training and certification of midwives, and the work of the visiting nurses. He urged the authorization of a dozen more visiting nurses whose work in educating parents in both the black and white neighborhoods had been successful.[33]

He also urged the city council to tighten regulations in the city's 686 stables and at the unsanitary public dumps where flies still bred. The city needed a new incinerator and closer protection of food supplies, especially of cooked foods in delicatessens. It also needed medical examinations for workers in restaurants, hotels, and other places that served food.[34]

Terry concluded by appealing for more tax dollars for public health. Good health was purchasable, he said, and more valuable than lower property taxes. Experts recommended one dollar per capita as a fair level of health protection. Seventy-five cents was the minimum. Jacksonville spent fifty cents. While the health of the community had been substantially improved, as indicated by the improved mortality rates, there still was a long way to go, especially for the black community. Terry urged health officials to press on with more dollars in their commitment to the growth of Jacksonville.[35]

□ The second area in which local government shaped urban growth was public education. In 1900 its policies reflected neglect: dingy classrooms, outdoor plumbing, low salaries that discriminated against women and blacks, and uncertified teachers. The governing body for Jacksonville's schools was an elected, three-person Duval County Board of Public Instruction. It in turn served under the authority of the state constitution, which required racial segregation and limited taxation to a maximum rate of five mills for local schools. The school board usually ran a deficit. The school superintendent, appointed by the board, influenced educational policies. At the turn of the century, he opposed compulsory education, which was the norm in most of the country. He also opposed free textbooks, because of the cost. Instead, in true Social Darwinian terms, he saw a voluntary system of education encouraging the "survival of the fittest" for the children of Jacksonville. Substantial support for public education did not characterize the city in 1900.[36]

Conditions did not change much in the ten years after the fire. In fact, they initially became worse because of the burning of three downtown schools. Scarce resources were diverted to rebuilding a brick, combined Central Grammar and Duval High School and "a large crude, three-story, frame" Stanton Middle School. (It became Stanton High School over the succeeding decade thanks to the efforts of its principal, James Weldon Johnson.) When schools opened in the fall of 1901, white students went on double sessions in Riverside and Springfield while black youngsters simply stayed home until their new facility opened the following January. The diversion of tax revenues to build the new schools led to a crisis in March 1903, when the school board had insufficient funds to complete the school year.[37]

Fons A. Hathaway, superintendent of schools, 1913–1921. Courtesy of the Florida State Archives.

To improve school finances, the Jacksonville Woman's Club began a campaign to increase the constitutional limitation on school funding from five to seven mills. The amendment, supported by the Duval delegation, passed the state legislature at the following session. To create interest and support for the public schools, the Woman's Club next organized Mothers Clubs, a forerunner of Parent-Teacher Associations. Its members also studied the need for kindergartens and compulsory education and supported the extension of the school term from five to eight months.[38]

Complicating attempts to fund the public schools was the great population growth in Jacksonville in the years following the fire. Enrollments increased almost 50 percent, from 6,765 students in 1900 to 9,861 ten years later. Three new elementary schools were built from tax revenues in an era before the state constitution made provision for bonding new construction. Secondary school enrollments more than doubled, and in 1906 the school board bought land to build a new Duval High School.[39]

Tax revenues increased during these years but not fast enough to cover expenses. Building maintenance was neglected. In 1906 the city Board of Health condemned the Central Grammar School building "due to the unsanitary condition of plumbing" in its lavatories. Classrooms were overcrowded and Fairfield parents urged construction of an addition to their school. Teachers' salaries increased only marginally, for black females not at all, despite an increased cost of living. In 1908 the Colored Woman's Club protested the absence of indoor plumbing and the inadequate maintenance of the Stanton School and its grounds. The school board promised relief, but the conditions persisted. By 1911 Stanton's roof leaked and the walls of the Oakland school for blacks were "in dangerous condition."[40]

Part of Stanton's problems reflected the school board's limited resources, but part also resulted from its discriminatory policies. The board subsidized white teachers attending state professional meetings, but not black teachers. It authorized an extra month of classes at the city's night school for whites, but not at Stanton. Money was available to increase the principal's salary at Duval High School, but not at Stanton. When a black elementary school requested an eight-month term comparable to the white school, the board turned it down. When another black school asked to open its facilities for a black Sunday School class, the board again said no, even though Sunday School classes met in white schools. While per-pupil expenditure for black students increased from $5.47 in 1900 to $19.07 in 1916–17, white expenditure rose from $12.04 to $86.99. Thus while black support increased almost four times in the generation after the Great Fire, white support increased more than seven times, leaving a greater gap between the two races at the end of the era.[41]

Less understandable was the relative decline in black enrollments over the years, because the black population remained a majority in the city (57 to 53 percent from 1900 to 1915). Where black youngsters comprised almost half the students in 1900, they numbered only one-third of the school population in 1916. White enrollments doubled over these years, while the black attendance increased only 50 percent. One can only assume either discouragement or discrimination contributed to the lower percentage of black scholars.

Meanwhile public opinion began to stir about the conditions of Jacksonville's schools. In 1910 Francis P. Conroy, the new president of the Board of Trade, the city's most influential body of business and professional men, spoke out about conditions in the schools. He found them "simply appalling." Jacksonville "should be ashamed," he said, "that such . . . dilapidated, unsanitary and unsatisfactory buildings" exist. Conroy met with school board officials after which the Board of Trade proposed a $400,000 bond issue for school construction. The school board and county commissioners endorsed the proposal, and the following spring the legislature passed a constitutional amendment authorizing bonding. Florida's voters ratified the amendment in 1912, and the Woman's Club began to mobilize public opinion for school improvements.[42]

Further progress came with the appointment of Fons A. Hathaway as superintendent of schools in 1913. Hathaway, the thirty-six-year-old principal of Duval High School, had been born in the Florida Panhandle and graduated from the University of Florida. Prior to moving to Jacksonville, he had been principal of Orlando High School. A professional educator active on both the state and national levels, Hathaway began a major effort to modernize the Duval County schools just at the time the state authorized increased funding to Florida counties.[43]

Hathaway began by focusing on instruction, encouraging teachers to attend what would now be called summer training institutes. At the time most elementary teachers had only high school diplomas. Hathaway also hired supervisors to assist less effective teachers. He persuaded the school board to require a college or normal school degree in order to teach high school. Hathaway then raised the minimum and maximum salaries three times over the next six years, introducing the system's first pay scale and across-the-board increases.[44]

The school board endorsed Hathaway's proposals. It expanded the curriculum, adding music, art, manual training, home economics, commercial courses, and special education classes for "backward or retarded pupils." It also introduced civics classes for elementary students and teacher training in high school. The board extended the school year to nine months and, following state legislative authorization in 1918, implemented compulsory education. To fund these programs the board depended on the expanding tax base of the county, plus a special one-mill tax for the urban district.[45]

New buildings were funded by a $1 million bond issue passed in 1915. Almost nine-tenths of the money went to build seven new elementary schools for white students and additions to other older schools. The board did allocate $115,000 to replace the frame structure at Stanton with a modern brick building as well as build three new elementary schools for blacks. Construction was delayed, first by the recession and then by the war. Still, Hathaway could report in early 1919 that the million-dollar program was practically complete, and "no city in the South . . . possessed an equal number of modern school plants."[46]

Earlier, Franklin H. Giddings, writing in *The Independent*, anticipated Hathaway's report: "At Jacksonville, Florida, the county superintendent of instruction, Mr. Fons A. Hathaway, in less than three years has obtained from the taxpayers the millions of dollars necessary to rebuild or remodel or re-equip according to the most modern plans, all the more important school buildings [*sic*], and to reorganize courses of instruction in a way to secure the enthusiastic confidence of a progressive community."[47]

Despite these efforts, the schools barely kept pace with the rapidly growing population. School enrollments increased another 50 percent, from 9,861 in 1910–11, to 14,909 in 1916–17 on the eve of World War I. Then the influx of war workers pushed enrollments up even further, leading once again to double sessions in 1918.[48]

Superintendent Hathaway's achievements in upgrading standards in public education, diversifying the curriculum, raising salaries, and building schools were substantial. They helped Jacksonville to begin catching up with other school systems across the country. Public support for the schools increased in the generation after the fire, as did the tax rate. The schools had entered the mainstream of middle-class life, contributing to the urban growth and development of this New South city.

Still, rapid population growth kept pressures on the system. As Duval High School once more became overcrowded in 1918, Hathaway began planning for two junior high schools. Economic resources never seemed to be quite enough to house and teach every youngster.

The unequal treatment of black pupils, teachers, and taxpayers was another problem. While segregated schools had been affirmed by the Supreme Court in *Plessy* v. *Ferguson* in 1890, the court had said *separate* and *equal*. In Jacksonville, as in other cities in the South and across most of the nation, equality did not exist. The educational system simply added to the legal, economic, and political subordination of black Americans.

□ Superintendent Hathaway and City Health Officer Terry represented the new breed of urban reformers in early twentieth-century America. Well educated and professionally active in their fields, they were experts who shaped portions of the urban environment. Both applied modern scientific standards to their respective fields. Terry changed Jacksonville from an unhealthy city, laying the foundations for contemporary public health practices. Hathaway brought Jacksonville's school system into the twentieth century, though on a more tenuous basis because of rapid population growth and limited resources. Terry achieved national recognition when the American Public Health Association met in Jacksonville in 1915. Hathaway received an honorary degree from the University of Florida for his contributions to public education on the local and state levels. Both

Hon. J. E. T. Bowden, mayor of Jacksonville, 1899–1901 and 1915–17. Reprinted from Rawls, *The Jacksonville Story*, 20.

eventually left Jacksonville, Terry moving to New York as health editor for a national magazine, Hathaway moving to Tallahassee in 1921, to serve in the administration of Governor John W. Martin.[49]

If individual leaders such as Terry and Hathaway shaped public policy in Jacksonville, they did not do so alone. Terry had the support of the city council most of the time as well as the mayor and the Board of Bond Trustees. Hathaway earned the support of the Duval County Board of Public Instruction as well as the Duval delegation to the state legislature.

These groups also played substantial roles developing public policies and shaping the character of the city during these years. In particular, the city council played an important part. It regulated passenger service on the street railways; forced the railroads to build viaducts or overpasses at corporate expense to separate vehicular and rail traffic; and initiated the efforts for a new passenger depot. It also segregated streetcars by race. Automobiles were another problem. As they increased in popularity, the council passed legislation in 1904 limiting their speed downtown to ten miles per hour. Cars must be licensed and have a "good horn" and two headlamps. No one under sixteen could drive in town. Five years later the council passed more legislation requiring vehicles to keep to the right and pass on the left. Drivers must use hand signals and yield to emergency vehicles. Later laws licensed drivers, limited downtown parking, and required parallel parking within six inches of the curb. While the council could not solve all of the problems resulting from the automobile, it laid the foundation for later public policy to control the use of the downtown streets.[50]

Jacksonville's mayors varied in their effectiveness in setting public policy. Duncan Fletcher was a strong mayor, both in the 1890s when he began a series of major public improvements and after the fire when he persuaded the council to put aside partisanship in the rebuilding of the city. His achievements locally and in the state Democratic party led to his election as United States senator in 1908.[51]

Another energetic mayor was Van C. Swearingen, elected in 1913. By then the transfer of executive power to the bond trustees had substantially weakened the mayor's office. Still, he called the charter convention that led to the governmental reorganization and the council-commission. Swearingen also rallied supporters in a campaign against vice. He began by ordering the police to clear the streets of prostitutes. Next he ordered them to keep minors out of pool halls and saloons. In addition, he condemned the romanticized giant paintings of nude women that hung over the bars in many turn-of-the-century taverns.[52]

Initially the mayor tried to isolate prostitution in the LaVilla section, west of town, but the LaVilla Civic League wanted the brothels out of their neighborhood. Then the Jacksonville Ministerial Alliance declared its support for closing all brothels. Swearingen agreed, provided employment was found for the women, and a week later gave orders to close down the red-light district effective June 1, 1914.[53]

The editors of the *Florida Times-Union* endorsed the action but voiced concern about the prostitutes simply scattering to other neighborhoods in the city. Apparently this happened because that fall, J. E. T. Bowden, former mayor of LaVilla and later of Jacksonville, challenged Swearingen for the office, attacking his anti-vice campaign on the grounds that the women had scattered and disrupted residential neighborhoods. Bowden's challenge led to an exciting spring election campaign. Progressive club women supported Swearingen and conservative men backed Bowden. Suddenly the campaign turned on charges by a former supporter that the mayor belonged to the Guardians of Liberty, a secret political group that was anti-Catholic and anti-Semitic. Traditionally, Jacksonvillians had substantial tolerance for Catholics and Jews. Rabbis and priests as well as laypeople were active participants in civic affairs. Morris Dzialynksi, lay leader of Congregation Ahavath Chesed, had been mayor and later was elected municipal court judge. Francis Conroy, a Catholic, had been elected president of the Board of Trade. As a result of these charges, the campaign became more heated. Bowden's victory with 58 percent of the vote provided some assurance that religious toleration prevailed. Subsequently Swearingen was appointed Florida's attorney general by the populist, demagogic, and anti-Catholic governor Sidney J. Catts.[54]

Mayor Bowden also played an activist role in office. A native of Spartanburg, South Carolina, the fifty-eight-year-old Bowden came to Jacksonville as a child after the Civil War. As a young man, he worked as a clerk in a mercantile business, later shifting his interest to real estate and politics. He served as mayor of LaVilla before its incorporation into Jacksonville in 1887 and twice as mayor of Jacksonville, from 1899 to 1901 and from 1915 to 1917. His daughter subsequently described him as "a firebrand who loved to politic, and enjoyed brass bands, bright lights and the company of theatrical people." During his second mayoral term after defeating Swearingen, Bowden took pride in his "liberal" administration, which encouraged an open city convivial to tourism, industrial development, and film production. He argued strongly for the new train station. He also promised fair play to African-Americans, restraining the police in the use of their guns and treatment of minorities. He suspended a police officer pending an investigation following the shooting death of a young black man. During the recession of 1915, he initiated cutbacks in government spending and looked for ways to assist the poor through city-county cooperation. His main thrust, however, was wooing the film industry to Jacksonville. His initial success brought substantial publicity to the city, but eventually it backfired. Critics rejected the excesses of some film stars as well as the frequency with which Bowden turned the city streets over to the filmmakers for chases, shootouts, and burnings. Filmmaking became the issue of the 1917 campaign and Bowden lost.[55]

The response to the mayoral leadership of Swearingen and Bowden pointed to a split in the Jacksonville white community. A substantial number of citizens wanted an open, tolerant city for business and pleasure. Another group wanted a moral city reflecting traditional Protestant Christian religious values. These people opposed not only prostitution but also gambling and the manufacture and sale of alcoholic beverages. They supported blue laws closing commercial establishments on the Sabbath. Further, many of them saw Catholics and Jews as threatening their traditional community values. Not all Jacksonvillians fit neatly into either camp. As views shifted from issue to issue, neither group dominated the community. What the two mayoral elections showed was the existence of a swing

St. Johns River (later Acosta) Bridge, completed in 1921. Courtesy of Wayne W. Wood.

group of voters shifting first in one direction and then another, generally avoiding extreme positions on either side.

□ Of all the public policies shaping the growth and character of Jacksonville before and after the turn of the century, local officials believed the actions of the United States Congress to deepen the St. Johns River channel were the most important. From the city's beginning, the river served as the primary avenue of transportation and commerce. Yet in the early years, ships crossing the bar at the mouth of the St. Johns River had a clearance of only three to five feet. Frequently they had to wait for high tide to sail upriver to Jacksonville. After the Civil War the newly formed Board of Trade petitioned Congress to build jetties at the river's mouth and cut through the bar. Congress appropriated funds in 1879 and the Corps of Engineers built the jetties. Yet the shallowness of the river channel still blocked entry for larger ships and limited Jacksonville commerce to coastal trade. In the early 1890s the Board of Trade persuaded the Duval County Commission to authorize $300,000 in bonds to dredge an eighteen-foot channel. That depth was still not sufficient, and the board petitioned once again in 1896 and secured congressional legislation in 1902 to dredge the channel to twenty-four feet.[56]

This project, completed by the Corps in 1907 at a cost of $2.1 million, marked a major breakthrough for Jacksonville shipping. It increased the volume and value of trade almost fourfold. The twenty-four-foot channel enabled the Cummer Lumber Company to build facilities to ship phosphates to Germany and England. It also attracted European ships to call at Jacksonville. Yet despite the improvement, larger European ships with their twenty-seven-foot drafts still had problems. They could load only partially at Jacksonville and then had to move on to other ports. Or they had to partially unload first at Charleston or Savannah before sailing on to Jacksonville. Colonel George Stallings, chief of the local Corps of Engineers, recommended a thirty-foot channel. Florida, he concluded, produced more naval stores than any other state, but could ship only limited amounts from Jacksonville because the channel was still too shallow. Again the Board of Trade lobbied Congress. Both Florida senators supported the petition. The Corps surveyed the river from its mouth to the city and passed its recommendations to the War Department and Congress. In 1910 Congress approved the thirty-foot channel.[57]

Funding for the deeper channel came in annual appropriations of $300,000 to $500,000. In early 1912 a delegation from the House Rivers and Harbors Committee came to Jacksonville to inspect the project. They discovered the entire city waterfront under private ownership and warned local officials to build municipal docks if they wanted further appropriations. More formally, the Corps put Jacksonville on notice that no more funds would be recommended for the harbor until the city agreed to operate its own docks, warehouses, and terminals to ensure that the state and public at large benefited from the federal appropriations.[58]

The Board of Trade responded quickly to this ultimatum by petitioning Governor Arthur Gilchrist and Florida legislators for a special session to authorize the city to bond and build a municipal facility. Tampa and Pensacola already had municipal terminals. The legislature responded by providing authorization. Following a publicity campaign developed by the Board of Trade and the media, Jacksonville voters endorsed the $1.5 million bond issue in January 1913. Construction followed, after selection of a board of port commissioners and a site out Talleyrand Avenue. The docks, the forerunner of the Jacksonville Port Authority, opened for shipping in 1915.[59]

Congressional determination that Jacksonville should have municipal docks clearly benefited the city's economy. It also pushed the city in a direction it had not intended to go, for local officials apparently had been satisfied with the railroads' near monopoly of the waterfront.

In addition to dredging the deep river channel and forcing Jacksonville to build municipal docks, the federal government maintained general oversight of the St. Johns River. It required changes along the waterfront following the 1901 fire to have Corps of Engineers approval. When St. Elmo Acosta proposed a vehicular bridge across the river prior to World War I, the Corps determined its site just east of the Florida East Coast Railroad bridge.

Because of the river and the Corps of Engineers' responsibility for it, the federal government played a major role in shaping the commercial development and character of Jacksonville. Its intervention previewed an increasingly broad range of federal policies affecting Jacksonville and other American cities during the two world wars and after.

□ The policies shaping the growth and development of Jacksonville from the fire to World War I came from both the private and public sectors. Local, state, and federal governments played important roles. Their impact, however, was uneven. On the one hand, they expanded areas of racial discrimination and virtually disfranchised black voters. On the other hand, they provided for improved black health care and education. State government made local government more accountable through an elected city commission. Gradually, too, the state also partially loosened its control over the city, allowing it to assert its authority to regulate local transportation, dairies, restaurants, food markets, and entertainment. Local governments, in turn, improved community health conditions and the schools. Mortality rates for both blacks and whites declined, and for the first time substantial numbers of Jacksonville residents extended their education beyond the eighth grade to high school. On the federal level, decisions to dredge the St. Johns River channel stimulated economic development. Federal policies also forced the city to establish some control over its port. As a result of public policy decisions, Jacksonville became more affluent, segregated, healthy, and regulated: all characteristics of New South cities and twentieth-century urban America.

FOUR

The Private Sector and Urban Growth

As early as 1835, our most perceptive foreign observer, Alexis de Tocqueville, described the role of voluntary associations in American life:

> Americans of all ages, all stations in life, and all types of disposition are forever forming associations. There are not only commercial and industrial associations in which all take part, but others of a thousand different types—religious, moral, serious, futile, very general and very limited, immensely large and very minute. Americans combine to give fetes, found seminaries, build churches, distribute books, and send missionaries to the antipodes. Hospitals, prisons, and schools take their shape in the same way. Finally, if they want to proclaim a truth or propagate some feeling by the encouragement of a great example, they form an association. In every case, at the head of any new undertaking, where in France you would find the government or in England some territorial magnate, in the United States you are sure to find an association.[1]

Jacksonville was no different. Residents volunteered their time and talents to a variety of community associations serving a wide range of interests. A few groups stood out in their contributions to shaping the character of this New South city. Among them were the Board of Trade/Chamber of Commerce, the Jacksonville Woman's Club, and the churches of the African-American community.

Formed in 1884, the Board of Trade became Jacksonville's premier business and civic organization. It comprised the leading white business and professional men of the city. Its goals included not only fostering trade, transportation, and manufacturing, but also collecting commercial statistics, resolving local business disputes, encouraging favorable local, state, and federal legislation, promoting business integrity, improving river navigation, and generally striving "with united effort to increase the wealth, industries, influence, trade and population of the City of Jacksonville and its suburbs." It also welcomed enterprising members from all sections of the country and all political persuasions.[2]

A more subtle goal was expressed by founding father and leading Jacksonville attorney, Colonel James Jacqueline Daniel. He welcomed the "men of force and energy" who were migrating to the city. They were "active and aggressive" entrepreneurs reflecting the "intense individualism" of Gilded Age business competition. Their rivalry, however, could work simply for their individual profits without regard for the city's welfare, or their efforts could be harnessed to advance theirs and the city's interest. Daniel saw the Board of Trade shaping "the active and enterprising individual factors to an effective and harmonious union," which advanced both personal interests and the prosperity of Jacksonville. In effect, the Board of Trade aspired to direct the economic development of Jacksonville.[3]

Its achievements prior to the fire were substantial. It successfully lobbied for reduced transportation rates, improved mail service, paved streets, a state railroad commission, and the establishment of a direct steamship line to New York. It protested increased insurance rates locally and, in 1891, prevented the abolition of the state board of health. Earlier it had drafted the 1887 municipal charter to expand the city's boundaries to include LaVilla, Fairfield, and East Jacksonville; opposed suspension of democratic government by the legislature in 1889; and then prepared the new charter passed in 1893, which included the introduction of the secret ballot, then considered a substantial voting reform. Most important for the city's development were the board's efforts to deepen the channel of the St. Johns River. First the board persuaded the state legislature to authorize Duval County to bond itself for the work, then it secured the approval of the county commission, and finally it obtained the support of the voters in an 1891 referendum. When the work to deepen the channel to eighteen feet was completed two years later, the board already had begun lobbying Congress for a deeper, twenty-four-foot channel. A state official observing the board's efforts called it "the most influential unofficial organization in the State of Florida."[4]

With this record, it is not surprising that board president Charles E. Garner called an emergency mass meeting of the community the day after the fire, and that Mayor Bowden and his city council members chose to join with the board's efforts, rather than vice versa. Board members directed the formation of the Jacksonville Relief Association with Garner at the helm. The rebuilding of Jacksonville owed much to their tradition of cooperative effort. Three years after the fire Richard H. Edmonds, editor of the regionally influential *Manufacturers' Record*, published in Baltimore, wrote of the spirit of Jacksonville so amply illustrated by the Board of Trade. It was alive, energetic, "always doing things for the advancement of the city."[5]

> Nowhere in the country have I heard more optimistic talk nor seen greater evidence of rapidly increasing prosperity than in Jacksonville. . . . The business men are alert and energetic. . . . [There] is a spirit of hustle and "go" which is doing things here, and which did things after the fire. . . . The whole place reminds one very strongly of the energy and the spirit of cooperation which, away back in the early eighties, gave Atlanta such a start that it has never since had time to slack up.[6]

The achievements of the board owed much to the eight-term presidency (1899–1907) of Captain Charles E. Garner. Born in Indiana, Garner moved to Jacksonville in 1881 at the age of twenty-eight. He worked first on the river as a steamboat captain, then he entered business in the city and later became a bank president. Information about his personal life is limited, but he worked hard, held the esteem of his board colleagues, advanced his own business career, and made a genuine contribution to the city. Under his leadership, the board successfully mediated strikes and the rail congestion that tied up the port in 1906–7. It supported bonding to the city's legal limit for more paved streets, water mains, sewers, bulkheads on the river, fire protection, and the construction of a city-county hospital. The board endorsed the building of the first paved road from South Jacksonville to the beaches, and when county officials could not agree on a route, Garner and two other civic leaders were asked to map the way. His board also oversaw the substantial economic growth in shipbuilding, fertilizer manufacturing, phosphate exports, railroad main-

Charles E. Garner, president of the Board of Trade, 1899–1907. Courtesy of the Haydon Burns Library.

tenance, and port expansion, which was stalled only temporarily by the recession of 1907.[7]

Throughout his terms as president, Garner never tried to take exclusive credit for the board's efforts in community development. Rather he believed "that no body of men . . . has worked harder, more unitedly, or with greater enthusiasm toward not only upbuilding the city, but of the entire state, than has the Jacksonville Board of Trade."[8]

Following the election of Francis B. Conroy as president in 1911, the board expanded its efforts in a new direction. Conroy, from Chicago, had come to Jacksonville for Armour and Company, and subsequently became a partner in a local meat packing firm. He saw economic development as part of a larger goal of civic progress. In addition to past support for better roads, a deeper river channel, and new business development, he urged board support to raise funds for a new St. Luke's Hospital; pass a state constitutional amendment to authorize bonding for new schools; and secure local public health measures to incinerate garbage, extend sewers, and pasteurize milk. Conroy particularly felt Jacksonville's schools were "appalling" and urged the elimination of "dilapidated, unsanitary and unsatisfactory buildings" by issuing bonds for new construction.[9]

Jacksonville Board of Trade. Courtesy of the Haydon Burns Library.

Under Conroy's successor, George L. Drew, son of a former governor and owner of a local lumber firm, the board responded to federal pressures for municipally owned docks by persuading Florida's governor to call a special session of the state legislature. When the governor stalled, the board offered to pay for the cost of the session. It next lobbied every state legislator to secure passage of authorization for a bond referendum and then campaigned successfully for the vote. Construction of the public docks was a prerequisite for Congress to release $500,000 to begin deepening the river channel to thirty feet, an issue the board also lobbied along with Florida's two senators (both board members) in Washington. The board encouraged the federation of the community's numerous neighborhood associations into a Central Civic Committee to lobby for civic improvements with the board's support and backed the first public relations film about the city, entitled *A Gay Time in Jacksonville*.[10]

In 1913 the board appointed a city planning committee chaired by architect Henry Klutho to draw up sketches for a civic center to include the City Hall, courthouse, armory, and post office as a first step toward a citywide plan. Civic centers clustering public buildings had been planned or built in Cleveland, Baltimore, and Washington, D.C. The board supported Jacksonville's becoming the motion picture capital of the East

Coast; endorsed building the new railroad station; and began the formation of a state Chamber of Commerce. The board further recommended construction of the first automobile bridge across the St. Johns River, but only after a bitter dispute over its location. Port and railroad interests feared the bridge might disrupt shipping. When bridge advocates threatened to secede if the board refused its support, the board endorsed the project with the strong proviso that the bridge not "unduly interfere" with the city's commerce.[11]

On the eve of the depression of 1914, the board renamed itself the Chamber of Commerce and published a book for national distribution about Jacksonville's great progress since the fire. The city's achievements were notable, and the board/chamber had played a major role not only in the economic development of the port, railroads, banking, insurance, new industry and commerce but also in support of public education, improved health conditions, park development, and community involvement. These business and professional men had combined their individual entrepreneurial interests with the larger goal of civic betterment to benefit, albeit unevenly, almost the entire community with jobs, homes, schools, shops, and recreational facilities.[12]

The depression of 1914–16, however, undercut Jacksonville's prosperity, and the effectiveness and unity of the chamber. Its annual reports referred to 1914 "as one of the most trying" years in memory, and "the year 1915 . . . [as] one in which our City has felt to a considerable degree the general depression caused by the European War." Exports in cotton, naval stores, lumber, and phosphates practically ceased.[13]

Evidence about the impact of the depression on the chamber's role as "the powerhouse" of Jacksonville comes in bits and pieces. Membership, which had increased over the preceding decade from about 400 to 1,150 in 1913, dropped 25 percent the following year with resulting financial pressures for the organization. No membership figures were listed for 1915. Chamber members, hard-pressed in their own businesses, had little extra time for community effort. Criticism of the chamber surfaced at a "self evaluation" banquet in February 1915. Mayor Bowden noted that, simply because of hard times, the chamber should not slow down. Chamber president Charles H. Mann, president of the Citizens' Bank of Jacksonville, saw the need for recruiting younger businessmen. Chamber secretary and treasurer George Leonard saw problems in trying to "loosen up the pocketbooks of many of the wealthier citizens." Apparently they had become more cautious in their support of public concerns. One board member complained that issues handed to committees too often died there. There was also talk that cutbacks in the chamber's role of publicizing Jacksonville nationally had hurt the city's image.[14]

Other factors also played a role in the chamber's decline. The generation of board/chamber leaders dating from the 1880s and 1890s had grown older. William B. Barnett, the city's premier banker, died in 1903. Wellington Cummer, the largest manufacturer in Duval County with his lumber mill and phosphate plant, and a strong supporter of board efforts, died in 1909. Florida East Coast Railroad president J. R. Parrott died in 1913. Captain Garner and board governor T. V. Porter followed in 1915. A new generation of chamber leaders had to take charge.

Another factor was the increasing specialization of work in early twentieth-century Jacksonville, as in other cities of the New South and nation. New business and professional associations, such as the Real Estate Board, Wholesale Grocers Association, and Advertising Federation, did not necessarily challenge the supremacy of the chamber, but they certainly pulled business and community energies in different directions. Following the self-evaluation of July 1915, chamber president Mann recommended the formation of a federation linking the many associations in the city. That August twenty-nine white groups, ranging from the Children's Home Society, Rotary, and Central Labor Council, to the bar association, medical society, taxpayers league, and port commission, formed an advisory council to work with the chamber on nonpartisan issues of public interest.[15]

Meanwhile, within the chamber, the Board of Governors planned a new membership campaign. Francis Conroy organized and launched it with a big rally in early April 1916. Chamber members were challenged to think about the spirit of the city, that spirit of cooperation, pride, and enthusiasm which makes a city great. On Sunday, April 8, clergy from Baptist, Methodist, and Presbyterian churches preached sermons on the responsibilities of citizenship and the "renewal of community conscience." Afterward, some 250 members set out to recruit every business and professional man in the community. By the end of the month, 1,516 new members had signed up. The slump had ended. New energies could be harnessed at the chamber to act for the city's interests as war clouds hovered on the horizon.[16]

Many observers of the New South rightly saw boards of trade and chambers of commerce as engines for economic development. They also welcomed northern capitalists and upheld white supremacy. Beyond that, Jacksonville's board/chamber worked for urban progress by supporting

Ninah May Holder Cummer, clubwoman, civic activist, and philanthropist. Reprinted from Daniel Pleasant Gold, *History of Duval County, Florida* (St. Augustine: The Record, 1928), 458.

better schools, public health, neighborhood parks, and community involvement. Thus it was more than just concerned with the business community's narrower goals of growth and profitability. Instead, it attempted to balance, in Colonel Daniel's words, individual interests with the community's welfare. By the standards of the late twentieth century, Jacksonville's board/chamber expressed elitist, sexist, and racist values. But in the context of cities across the United States in those years, these attitudes were not unique. Of significance was the energy expended successfully moving the city into the modern age.

In 1911 a *Florida Times-Union* editorial asked:

> What organization does the most to make this city what it should be? We are not asking now, what does the most to increase its size, its business, its worth. To this the answer would unquestionably be the Board of Trade. But what organization does the most to shape the character of the city—morally, educationally, aesthetically? Unquestionably the Woman's Club; and since character is more important than size we must rate the Woman's Club first among organizations in Jacksonville.[17]

In January 1897 about forty women met in the parlors of the Windsor Hotel downtown to organize a Woman's Club. Their efforts reflected steps taken by middle- and upper-class white women in towns and cities across the country in the 1880s and 1890s. In part these women were the beneficiaries of their growing numbers and the prosperity of urban life where maids, housekeepers, and nurses relieved them of much of the household work. They also had smaller families, better health care, ready-made clothes, and canned food, resulting in more time to become engaged in other activities. Initially, churches had provided an outlet for female energies, supporting both home and foreign missionary societies. Methodists particularly were active in starting schools and hospitals for poor people, both black and white. An Atlanta Methodist woman became the first person to organize a settlement house in the nation, four years before Jane Addams's Hull House opened in Chicago. From church-related activities, New South women, like their northern counterparts, joined the fight against the excesses of strong drink, first through supporting temperance and later through the advocacy of abstinence and prohibition in the Women's Christian Temperance Union. The clubs came next. Women frequently were denied access to advanced education and initially came together in the clubs to read and discuss books. In the process, they began to build social networks and then to broaden their horizons in concern for the education, health, and welfare of their communities. As historian Anne Firor Scott has written, "from literary subjects the women moved rather quickly to social concerns."[18]

In Jacksonville the club organizers followed in the footsteps of the women who had founded St. Luke's Hospital in 1873, the Jacksonville Library Association in 1877, and the Ladies' Friday Musicale two decades later. From its beginning the Woman's Club had a literary focus, a social orientation, and philanthropic concerns. In its first year the women established reading and study groups, heard visiting speakers, hosted a reception and banquet at the Windsor Hotel, and employed a visiting nurse to attend indigent patients. The club grew rapidly, attracting the few business and professional women of the city as well as the wives and daughters of Jacksonville's business and professional men. It also affiliated with the Florida Federation of Women's Clubs and the national General Federation of Women's Clubs. Over the succeeding years while the literary and social aspects continued, the philanthropic efforts of the Woman's Club grew rapidly. Their concerns included the public schools of the community, health care, child welfare, women's issues, and the poor.[19]

Initially, the main concern was educational. The club women brought Jabez Lamar Monroe Curry to Jacksonville in 1900. Georgia-born, Harvard-trained, a disciple of Horace Mann, the nation's leading antebellum advocate of universal education, Curry also was a Civil War veteran, Baptist minister, lawyer, professor, and college president. He went to Jacksonville as the general agent of the Peabody Education Fund for improving southern education and chairman of the Committee on Education of the Slater Fund for Negro education. Curry crusaded for public education as "the cornerstone" of the New South, "a universal right," and "the fundamental basis of general and permanent prosperity." His severe criticism of Jacksonville's public schools helped the Woman's Club to prioritize education on their agenda of concerns.[20]

Their approach to school reform took several directions. First was greater public funding. Having kept the schools open with an emergency $1,000 gift in 1900, the club women realized private funding was not a permanent solution. They successfully lobbied the state legislature in 1903 to raise the constitutional limits for spending on public education from five to seven mils. Later they initiated legislative efforts to authorize bonding to build new schools.[21]

A second approach anticipated the creation of Parent-Teachers Associations. In 1903 Ada Cummer, wife of Jacksonville's largest manufacturer, and her daughter-in-law, Nina, formed the first Mother's Club in Jacksonville. Its purpose was to involve mothers in their children's schooling through monthly meetings with their teachers. A by-product sought to foster general interest in the local schools and encourage their physical maintenance and well-being. Each school eventually had its Mother's Club.[22]

A third direction lay in the formation of the Jacksonville Kindergarten Association for free kindergartens, especially for poor children. Again Ada Cummer along with the mayor's wife, Anna Louise Fletcher, played major roles.[23]

Following the resignation of the county school superintendent in 1905,

May Mann Jennings, club-woman, conservationist, feminist, and civic activist. Courtesy of the Florida State Archives.

the club women launched a campaign to appoint a woman superintendent. They believed Mattie Rutherford, principal of Jacksonville Elementary School, was eminently qualified, and petitioned Governor Broward to that effect. Opponents claimed that women were not eligible for the position, and the governor appointed an old friend recommended by his political advisors.[24]

A major expansion of the club's activities came in 1906 with the formation of the Social Science Class. Meeting biweekly from September through May, it studied civil service reform, child labor, compulsory education, pure food, juvenile courts, and public kindergartens for all schools. A key figure in this development was May Mann Jennings, wife of Governor William Sherman Jennings (1901–5), who moved to Jacksonville after her husband's term of office.

Biographer Linda Vance called May Jennings "Florida's most impressive and successful female citizen . . . matched by few other figures in Florida history, male or female." She lived for ninety-one years, spending sixty of them in public life. Most remembered as an environmentalist (then called a conservationist) and for saving the Everglades, she worked through the women's clubs and Florida Federation to lobby city council, state legislature and Congress for reforms that included education, public health, prisons, child labor, juvenile courts, prohibition, and woman's suffrage.[25]

Personally, May Jennings resembled her father, Austin Mann, a restless, successful businessman who moved to Florida from New Jersey in 1873, attracted by the state's tropical beauty and the chance to invest in citrus groves. The family settled in remote Crystal River of Hernando County where Mann grew oranges, practiced law, published a newspaper, and entered state politics as a liberal. The daughter inherited her father's restlessness, vitality, optimism, and love of politics. She also developed an appreciation of her rural, natural environment. May attended convent school in St. Augustine after her mother died. She was an excellent student, self-motivated, articulate, and inquisitive. Upon graduation, she helped her father in his political career, where she met and married attorney William Sherman Jennings. From Illinois, Jennings was a cousin of the popular three-time presidential candidate William Jennings Bryan. The latter's personal support combined with effective politicking by both husband and wife led to Jennings's nomination and election as governor of Florida in 1900.[26]

Following the governor's term in Tallahassee, the family moved to Jacksonville. May Jennings joined with the Cummer women, Lina Barnett (wife of Bion H., son of the founder of Barnett Bank who died in 1903), Annie Broward (the governor's wife), Jessie Atkinson Ball (the *Florida Times-Union* editor and publisher's wife), and others to awaken this New South city to concerns beyond economic growth and development. Their efforts included community education as they welcomed Florence Kelley of the National Consumers League, New York journalist Jacob Riis (presenting a speech entitled "The Battle of the Slums"), J. Horace McFarland of the American Civic Association, Owen Lovejoy of the National Child Labor Committee, Jane Addams of Hull House, suffragist Anna Shaw, as well as state and local officials and experts to speak in public lectures on issues of public concern. The women organized classes with recommended reading lists for the approximately 280 members of the club examining the juvenile court system, child labor conditions, "the city and its problems," municipal ownership, public health, public schools, city

The Woman's Club of Jacksonville. Courtesy of Wayne W. Wood.

jails, and public charities. Over the succeeding several years, the Social Science Class became virtually the steering committee for the Woman's Club's community activities.[27]

An early concern was tuberculosis, the number one killer of the era. Jacksonville and Florida lacked any sanitaria or medical provisions to combat the dread disease. The Woman's Club initiated a tuberculosis exhibit to help educate the community; helped finance and organize a tuberculosis camp to isolate and provide medical assistance for a handful of white men; lobbied the City Council successfully for a contagious disease wing at the new St. Luke's Hospital; and lobbied the state legislature unsuccessfully for a state sanitarium. While the camp had funds to accommodate only a few white males, many of whom recovered and returned to work, the club women saw its value as a continuing reminder for greater state action.[28]

The women built a club house in 1904 on East Duval Street downtown and welcomed charitable groups in the city to use its meeting facilities. Informally, then actively, they encouraged cooperation and communication between the groups and in 1910 initiated the creation of Associated Charities. This new organization reflected the drive for efficiency and organization in the Progressive Era. It sought to eliminate waste, duplication, and "indiscriminate giving," in part to make limited resources stretch further and in part to prevent fraudulent applications or the giving of excessive assistance.[29]

The association also reflected the latest "methods and ideals of modern philanthropy." Consultants from the Russell Sage Foundation visited Jacksonville to help in its organization. The association trained social workers to investigate and work with recipients, in some cases to enable a person to return to self-dependence. It encouraged children to stay in school, found jobs for employable people, removed children from unsavory homes, and prosecuted delinquent husbands. It recognized the variety of causes for individual problems that reflected at times human weakness, bad local conditions, or a disruptive environment. While the emphasis was on helping white residents in trouble, Associated Charities did hire Eartha M. M. White, a local black schoolteacher, to provide limited assistance to the African-American community. Waldo Cummer, a son of the prominent business and civic family, served as one of the association's first presidents. Support came from a range of business and professional men and women as well as their spouses. An advisory committee brought together representatives from women's clubs as well as the major white Protestant denominations, Catholics, Unitarians, and Jews. In his first annual report, Association General Secretary V. R. Manning wrote, "The Woman's Club blazed the trail in this social advance."[30]

Following a visit from the president of the General Federation of Women's Clubs in 1910, Jacksonville's club women reorganized their committee structure into departments for greater effect. They expanded their art, music, literature, and household economics departments as well as the departments devoted to various aspects of social work. For example, the Civics Department initiated the formation of a city Playground Commission composed of citizens from several municipal, civic, and philanthropic organizations. It also persuaded the city council to hire supervisors and equip two parks with playground apparatus.

A Conservation Department reflected increasing environmental concerns on the part of the club women. Their letters supporting a cross-Florida canal as part of the development of inland waterways may seem mistaken by late twentieth-century standards, but not then. The women also encouraged the observance of Arbor Day in the schools with appropriate tree-planting ceremonies. Subsequent efforts led to an emphasis on bird preservation, cooperation with the Florida Audubon Society, support for the creation of Florida's first state park in the Everglades, and lobbying for the appointment of a state forester.[31]

The Education Department worked for closer parent–teacher–school board cooperation as well as for physical improvements in the public schools. Later it worked closely with the Board of Trade, lobbying aggressively for a state constitutional amendment to authorize bonding for school construction. Afterward, they rallied voters to secure passage of a million-dollar bond referendum.

The Industrial and Social Conditions Department raised public consciousness in support of passing juvenile court and child labor bills, while the Legislative Department lobbied directly, and encouraged club members to write their representatives. While the child labor bill failed to pass its first two times, the club women did succeed in achieving the creation of a juvenile court system, increased appropriations for the state reform school, prohibition of local horse racing and gambling, and public school funding. They also encouraged letters to Congress on behalf of the General Federation's agenda.

Finally, the Public Health Department sold Christmas seals to raise money for the tuberculosis camp, employed a visiting nurse in cooperation with Associated Charities, and supported city efforts for pure milk, the banishment of flies from bakeries and restaurants, and the elimination of common drinking cups in stores. This department also sponsored educational programs on public health as well as the annual meeting of Associated Charities, graduation exercises for the nurses' training class at St. Luke's Hospital, and the organizational meeting to establish a YWCA in Jacksonville. In subsequent years it also helped in the formation of the Travelers' Aid Society, the Society for the Prevention of Infant Mortality as well as civic and women's clubs in Springfield and South Jacksonville. Setting the agenda for the community efforts of the club was the Social Science class formed in 1906. It met biweekly, invited speakers to raise social issues, and provided the catalyst for community action.[32]

With the coming of motion pictures to Jacksonville, the club women voiced concern about their content, particularly for children. In 1912 the Legislative Department, reflecting the Sabbatarian proclivities of its white middle-class membership, persuaded the mayor and city council to pass an ordinance closing all theaters, vaudeville shows, and movies on Sundays. A court injunction blocked its enforcement pending judicial review, and subsequently theaters were closed only from 6:30 to 8:30 P.M. on Sundays so as not to compete with evening church services. Through its actions, the Civics Department became the unofficial censor for motion pictures in Jacksonville.[33]

For the biennial legislative session of 1913, the club women returned to the issue of child labor. They began by hosting the annual meeting of the National Child Labor Committee in Jacksonville to publicize the bill. They arranged public meetings throughout the community, and Maymie Corbett (wife of Prudential Insurance Company manager Walter Corbett) even arranged to have sermons preached on the subject in "all the churches of the city." Once the child labor law was passed, the Industrial and Social Conditions Department provided volunteers to help state officials enforce the law by reporting violations.[34]

In a less publicized manner, the club women undertook to make employment more bearable, particularly for working women. Early in the century, they opened the second floor of their clubhouse for downtown working women to lunch, sit down, and rest before returning to their jobs. They encouraged employers to provide stools for sales girls in their shops, and checked to see whether they paid their clerks extra for night work during the Christmas holidays. They also began providing hot lunches for high school children who lived too far to return home for their midday meal, and hot suppers for night school students.[35]

In February 1909 the club women became aware of the inadequacies of the Duval County jail, popularly known as Raspberry Park. May Jennings led a delegation of club women and city council members to the facility. The jail consisted of two rooms: one forty by five feet in size housing sixty-seven black men, the other, twenty by five feet, with seventeen white men. According to their report, "Neither cell had cots, windows or plumbing. Inmates slept on the stone floor, winter and summer, surviving on bread and water once a day and corned beef on Sunday. The city's health officer had never visited the place." The women were outraged and Jennings successfully urged the city council to appropriate $967 to add plumbing, larger cells, and windows. Still not satisfied, the women eventually persuaded the council to condemn the building and construct a county prison farm north of the city.[36]

By the middle of the second decade after the fire, the Woman's Club had reached a plateau. Still numbering between 280 and 290 women, it lost some members to death and other departures, while gaining newcomers. Their range of existing responsibilities seemed almost too numerous to allow for new ventures. Thus their education committee, instead of initiating new proposals, supported the work of Fons A. Hathaway, the progressive superintendent of schools. The public health committee worked closely with Dr. Charles Terry and his successors at City Hall. The legislative and civics committees cooperated with initiatives by the Board of Trade and other organizations including the YWCA, Red Cross, Children's Home Society, St. Luke's Hospital, Boy's Home, Seaman's Mission, Federation of Mothers' Clubs, Infant Welfare Association, Springfield Improvement Association, and State Anti-Tuberculosis Association. Many of these groups the club women had helped form and support with financial contributions. They also funded scholarships to the State Woman's College in Tallahassee and helped organize relief for Syrian war refugees coming to join Jacksonville's growing Middle Eastern, primarily Lebanese, community. They lobbied for a woman's building at the county prison farm, slaughterhouse legislation from the city council, a children's program at the movie theaters, Royal Palm State Park in the legislature, and the federal Keating-Owen Child Labor bill through their local congressman and senators. Particularly noteworthy in the second decade were May Jennings's efforts to work with Eartha White and the black Federation of Women's Clubs on issues of mutual concern. Finally, the club women participated in the growing feminist movement of the Progressive Era where women assumed increasing responsibility for their own lives, along with the moral obligation of service to their communities.[37]

The depression slowed the growth and development of the Woman's Club in 1914–15. The proliferation of other community service organizations doubtless took away potential members and support from the community. After the formation of the Springfield Improvement Association (later the Springfield Woman's Club) in the suburb where May Jennings lived, she increasingly divided her time among it, the Woman's Club, and the Florida Federation. Annie Broward had to budget her time among managing the Jacksonville Towing and Wrecking Company, her late husband's business, the Woman's Club, YWCA, and serving as the first woman appointed to the Duval County School Board. When the war came to the United States in 1917, the club women put many projects on hold, such as the plan for a dental clinic for children, in order to support the war effort.[38]

Still, by almost any standard of measurement, the club women in Jacksonville accomplished a great deal between the fire and World War I. In almost every area of social concern, other than race relations, the club provided leaders and workers, persuading male-dominated organizations to respond to their agendas. Francis P. Conroy of the Board of Trade voiced the enlightened male view when introducing Horace McFarland of the America Civic Association: "I cannot speak too highly of the position taken by the Woman's Club of this city in the matter of civic improvement. They have always been leaders in anything looking to the betterment of our streets, parks and public buildings. . . ." He could have added schools, health care, the environment, and any community institution that worked to improve the quality of life in the city. In effect, as women's clubs across the region and nation contributed to the quality of urban development during these years, Jacksonville's white middle-class women also played a substantial and often leading role in the development of Jacksonville as a New South city.[39]

□ For African-Americans in Jacksonville, the shape of their New South city came largely from the ideas and practices of Booker T. Washington. Born a slave in Virginia, and encouraged by northern whites in his education before, during, and after attending Hampton Institute, a school for blacks established in eastern Virginia after the Civil War, Washington internalized the values of hard work, sobriety, thrift, and self-help in the New South creed. In founding Alabama's Tuskegee Institute he, as much as J. L. M. Curry, saw education as the means to economic advancement. Washington also hoped that economic advancement for African-Americans would mean acceptance by white Americans. Here he achieved success only within the framework of the white supremacy doctrines of the region. Personally he was welcomed and praised by white and black Floridians when he toured the state in 1912. And within limits, individual Jacksonville blacks, such as Joseph E. Lee and James Weldon Johnson, received personal recognition when admitted to the Florida bar. But these achievements did not prevent disfranchisement, Jim Crow laws, and even lynchings when white southerners saw fit. As a result, building a New South for blacks meant working within the confines of a city and state in which opportunities were limited by both custom and law. Yet within these confines, Jacksonville's black community made substantial progress through the work of both individuals and associations.[40]

The most influential black voluntary association in Jacksonville, as in other minority communities across the nation, was the church. In 1900 twenty-five Baptist, one Presbyterian, and twenty-three Methodist churches served black Jacksonville. Many of these churches were tiny, with just a handful of members, but a few, like Bethel Baptist Institutional Church, Mt. Zion African Methodist Episcopal Church, and Ebeneezer Methodist Episcopal Church, played major roles in the city's growth and development.[41]

Bethel Baptist was the largest, oldest, and wealthiest black church in Jacksonville. Its origins dated from before the Civil War when four whites with their two slaves founded it. After the war, in a practice common in many biracial congregations across the South where black members com-

Bethel Baptist Institutional Church. Courtesy of the Haydon Burns Library.

prised a majority, the whites separated to form their own First Baptist Church.[42]

To the Bethel congregation in 1892 came one of the outstanding ministers of the era, the Reverend J. Milton Waldron. Born in 1863, Waldron had been educated at Lincoln University and Newton Theological Institute, both in the North. Initially a follower of Booker T. Washington, he began to build at Bethel a center for African-American achievement. The church already supported the Florida Baptist Academy, a high school for blacks, who lacked access to public secondary education in Jacksonville at that time. In 1894 Waldron incorporated Bethel as the first black institutional church in the South. This expansion of roles, one that urban Prot-

Rev. J. Milton Waldron, pastor of Bethel Baptist Institutional Church, 1892–1907. Courtesy of the Eartha White Collection, University of North Florida.

estant churches in the North were taking to reach out to their surrounding communities as a part of the Social Gospel, enabled Bethel to provide social services to the community, industrial training, a Bible institute, and a tract publishing company.[43]

Waldron next led the congregation in building a brick facility to house the new programs and worship services. Members took pride in its construction by "colored mechanics under the direction of colored contractors." The completed building included a sanctuary seating 1,150 and nine classrooms. Many saw it as the "most convenient and attractive building in the city." The fire destroyed this new facility, and Waldron then led the congregation in rebuilding a church that in the late twentieth century still stands at 1058 Hogan Street. It is one of the more handsome and distinctive buildings in downtown Jacksonville. This new facility expanded its services further, adding a kindergarten, young men's club, dining room, reading room and library, bath and toilet rooms for both men and women, print shop, and a room for social and indoor sports.[44]

Meanwhile Waldron undertook new ventures. In January 1901 he joined with the pastor of Mt. Zion AME Church and six others to form

Eartha M. M. White, teacher, social worker, businesswoman, clubwoman, and civic activist. Courtesy of the Eartha White Collection, University of North Florida.

what became the Afro-American Life Insurance Company to provide burial benefits for the black community. The company also opened a savings department through which individuals could deposit ten, fifteen, or twenty-five cents per week. There were no black banks in Jacksonville then.[45]

In 1905 Waldron welcomed President Theodore Roosevelt to Jacksonville at Florida Baptist Academy as part of the President's southern tour. Six thousand black and white citizens heard the President praise the school's achievements and exhort his listeners to pursue their education, be thrifty, own their homes, and raise good families.[46]

Waldron left Jacksonville in 1907 to assume the pastorate of Shiloh Baptist Church in Washington, D.C. Whether he left for greater opportunity or whether the changing, more restrictive social environment of Jacksonville pushed him out is unknown. Evidence does point, however, to Waldron becoming more impatient and intolerant of Booker T. Washington's policies of accommodation with white supremacy. In the nation's capital, Waldron became a member of the Niagara Movement with W. E. B. DuBois in 1907 and, two years later, one of the founders of the National Association for the Advancement of Colored People (NAACP), an organization committed to challenging white supremacy.[47]

Waldron's departure did not end Bethel's role in Jacksonville. Under his successor, the Reverend John E. Ford, Bethel continued to serve as a social, educational, cultural, and political center for the community. Ford, from Chicago, previously had pastored churches in Los Angeles and Denver. His Jacksonville tenure lasted from 1907 to 1943. It was during Ford's ministry that Bethel member Eartha M. M. White made many of her substantial contributions to the African-American community.[48]

Eartha White, born in 1876, attended public schools in Jacksonville and then Florida Baptist Academy. She also studied music and dance in New York, returning to Jacksonville in 1896. During the Spanish-American War, White became one of the "colored nurses" caring for sick soldiers. The following year she obtained a teaching appointment in a one-room, rural school at Bayard in Duval County. In 1901 she was transferred to Stanton School in Jacksonville. A follower of Booker T. Washington, White had joined the National Negro Business League at its formation in 1900, and probably helped organize the Jacksonville chapter in 1907. White also worked part time for the new Afro-American Life Insurance Company. Following the fire, she helped with the relief work for blacks made homeless by the conflagration. She also became involved, after attending a meeting at Bethel, in revitalizing the Union Benevolent Association, a group formed in 1875 to provide assistance for poor blacks. It did not become operative until White, assisted by her mother, solicited funds to build a Colored Old Folks' Home, which opened in 1902. White became president of the home and its primary fund raiser.[49]

From her position as president of the Colored Old Folks' Home, White helped organize a City Federation of Women's Clubs, which by 1916 comprised sixteen groups including the colored YWCA, the Brooklyn Improvement Club, the J. H. Blodgett Improvement Club (named after the prominent black contractor), the Old Folks' Home, and the M. E. Smith Club (named after its founder and organized in 1896). The federation, like the (white) Woman's Club of Jacksonville, had departments concerned with the condition of young women, children, health and hygiene, domestic science, the social sciences, business, suffrage, education, temperance, juvenile courts, art, music, religion, and literature. It helped establish the first playground in the black community, improvements for the county jail, the first social worker in the black community, and two school nurses for black schools. It also worked with the white women's clubs; participated in community celebrations, such as Emancipation Day as well as Lincoln's, Washington's, and Frederick Douglass's birthdays; and became the first black organization to be admitted as a delegate member of the American

Mt. Zion A.M.E. Church. Courtesy of Wayne W. Wood.

Red Cross. Surviving documents in White's papers do not directly say it, but their presence suggests that White was probably involved in all of these accomplishments. She also helped organize a State Federation of Colored Women in 1909. When the Woman's Club sparked the formation of Associated Charities in 1910, White became their first black "friendly visitor," assisting needy people in the black community. Her efforts as a social worker, club woman, educator, and church member did not prevent her from also engaging in business ventures and lobbying local politicians for parks and other programs for her people. Her efforts helped Jacksonville African-Americans to develop a richer, broader community life.[50]

The accomplishments of Bethel Baptist Institutional Church and its members were not unique to Jacksonville's religious community. Mt. Zion AME Church under its pastor, the Reverend Elias J. Gregg, also played a substantial role. Mt. Zion sponsored Edward Waters College, a struggling small institution training teachers and clergy, which moved to Jacksonville in the early 1890s. The fire destroyed both its buildings and Mt. Zion AME Church. Rebuilding the church began in 1902. Its handsome brick sanctuary still stands in the late twentieth century. The college, however, lacked adequate funds, renting space first in a public elementary school and then settling at the Odd Fellows Temple for several years. In 1907 trustees purchased the college's current site northwest of downtown on Kings Road, but construction of its main building, Centennial Hall, under the direction of black architect Richard L. Brown, was not completed until 1916. The new president, arriving in 1913, did not wait for the building to be completed. Kansas-born and educated at the state university, the Reverend John A. Gregg served as a missionary in South Africa and pastored churches in his home state and Missouri before coming to Jacksonville. At Edward Waters he raised academic standards, provoking protests from the parents of students who had to repeat courses. Athletic fields were cleared and Edward Waters teams competed, despite inadequate equipment, with Florida Baptist and Cookman Institute in football, baseball, and other sports. Gregg stayed in Jacksonville for seven years, then was appointed president of Wilberforce University and later AME Bishop in Cape Town, South Africa.[51]

A third church playing a substantial part in black Jacksonville's growth and development was Ebeneezer Methodist Episcopal Church, organized after the Civil War and affiliated with the northern branch of the Methodist Church. It became the local sponsor of the Cookman Institute, founded in 1872 as the first private high school for blacks in Florida. Both Ebeneezer and Cookman burned in the fire also. Northern funding enabled Cookman to be rebuilt with minimal delay, and the new facility opened in 1905. Its enrollment of 372 students came mostly from Florida and Georgia.[52]

Cookman's faculty included in roughly equal numbers southern black teachers and Methodist teacher-missionaries from the North. Its curriculum contained college preparatory courses in the sciences, mathematics, foreign languages, and literature as well as vocational courses in shoemak-

Centennial Hall, Edward Waters College. Courtesy of Wayne W. Wood.

ing, tailoring, agriculture, printing, and home economics. Contemporaries considered Cookman the best of the private black schools in Jacksonville, and alumni remembered it with considerable affection. Its most famous graduate was A. Philip Randolph, founder of the Sleeping Car Porters Union and outstanding twentieth-century civil rights leader. Randolph graduated from Cookman in 1907 and then worked in Jacksonville in a series of jobs collecting weekly insurance premiums, clerking in a grocery store, driving a delivery wagon for a drug store, stacking logs in a lumberyard, and pushing a wheelbarrow in a fertilizer factory. Randolph refused to follow his father into the ministry of an AME church, but instead became converted by the vision of W. E. B. DuBois in his famous book, *The Souls of Black Folk*. Recognizing that the South offered little future to a believer in equal rights for blacks, Randolph, like an increasing number of Jacksonville's best and brightest, headed North in 1911.[53]

Another prominent member of Ebeneezer ME Church was James Weldon Johnson, teacher, poet, novelist, politician, statesman, and civil rights leader. Born in Jacksonville in 1871, Johnson came from a strong family. His Virginia-born father had been a free black before the Civil War, who came to Jacksonville via New York City and Nassau to become a headwaiter at one of the city's resort hotels. Johnson's Bahamian-born mother taught school and directed the church choir. Together the parents provided their children with music, books, and other middle-class goods and values. The younger Johnson graduated from Jacksonville's Stanton Colored School with a reputation as "a steady cool-headed boy—a boy that weighed things, found out what he wanted, and waited his turn." He next attended Atlanta University, where after his graduation in 1894, he returned to become principal at Stanton, one of the highest status positions for a black in Jacksonville.[54]

At Stanton, Johnson proceeded to expand the elementary school's curriculum to include high school subjects. By 1903 he had created Florida's first black high school. Johnson also started a weekly newspaper where he affirmed the principles of Booker T. Washington: hard work, education, achievement, and self-worth. He also affirmed Jacksonville, writing in 1895 that the city was "regarded by colored people all over the country as the most liberal town in the South." That feeling did not last. Increasingly, he saw the barriers of Jim Crow descend. With other community leaders, he protested the city council's passage of an ordinance segregating streetcars. Following the fire, Johnson was almost shot by militia as he walked and talked with a northern black female journalist who had Caucasian features. By 1903 he knew it was time to leave. Jacksonville had too few opportunities and too much racial hostility.[55]

While the northern Methodist church sponsored Cookman Institute, the Woman's Home Missionary Society of the Methodist Episcopal Church, South, in 1886 established Boylan Industrial Home and School, one of fifteen such schools they sponsored for black girls in the South. It primarily prepared young women for teaching or domestic vocations. In 1901 Boylan established a nurses' training program. Its purposes were twofold: to relieve suffering and to furnish young women with another career opportunity. Initially the school operated without a hospital, and students practiced their skills doing home visits. Following the fire, seventy-five victims, most suffering from infectious diseases, sought care at the school, which was converted into a makeshift hospital. By the end of the year, patients regularly sought medical care at the school's two-room infirmary. In 1902 a New England widow donated $1,500 in memory of her husband to secure land and a building for a hospital. Two years later Brewster Hospital and its nursing school accommodated up to fifteen patients. Black physicians could take patients there, perform operations, teach student nurses, and obtain qualified nurses to do home care. Although minimally funded, it was the only hospital where black doctors could practice in Jacksonville, and it had strong community support from church women.[56]

Clearly church support and involvement played a major role in developing educational opportunities for Jacksonville's blacks, improving health care, and even starting businesses. But the churches were not alone. Characteristic of the era in both the black and white communities was the cooperation or interdependence of people and institutions. J. Milton Waldron pastored Bethel Baptist and started an insurance company. Eartha White was a club woman, social worker, teacher, and businessperson. Joseph Blodgett was a successful contractor who supported White's social work, the National Negro Business League, the Methodist church, and Edward Waters College. The black masonic temple was home to a bank, pharmacy, law offices, and other enterprises. The barriers between business, religion, politics, culture, and community seemed less impenetrable than in later times. The members of the city's National Negro Business League chapter came from diverse backgrounds and reflected these connections. Information about the Jacksonville chapter is sketchy, but probably it provided a meeting ground for black business owners and managers. It also encouraged economic development. In March 1912 the local chapter hosted Booker T. Washington. The internationally famous African-American was introduced by George Bedell, a local white attorney and member of the Duval County School Board, and spoke to an audience of 2,500 blacks and whites.[57]

Over the course of the fifteen years following the fire, black business growth and development was substantial. Most of the black businesses listed in the city directories for those years, however, were small retail operations, or artisans and handicrafters providing a service. Their numbers grew. Retail groceries increased from forty-three to seventy-three, meat markets from five to seventeen, restaurants from nineteen to twenty-nine, saloons from one to twelve, wood yards from one to thirteen, and undertakers from none to four. Despite the advent of the automobile, blacksmiths increased from four to twelve. Though black barbers lost ground to immigrant barbers in northern cities, Jacksonville's tonsorial specialists increased from nineteen to fifty-eight. Dressmakers, furniture repairers, bicycle repair shops, shoemakers, and cabinetmakers also increased in number.[58]

In addition, there were more professional people. The number of physicians increased from six to twenty-two. In 1900 there were no black dentists. Fifteen years later there were four. Lawyers increased from three to eight. More impressive were the efforts at establishing newspapers (there were three weeklies in 1915), banks (there were two in 1910 and one in 1915), insurance companies (two in 1915), real estate firms (from none to six), and movie theaters (from none in 1900 to three in 1915).[59]

The small size and limited capital of Jacksonville's black businesses made success difficult. By 1919 the only black bank had capital of about

$250,000 compared with the Barnett Bank's millions, and it did not survive the 1920s. The newspapers were weeklies compared with the daily *Florida Times-Union* and *Metropolis*, and also did not survive. The real estate firms were small operations, not comparable to Stockton and Company, and the theaters were small. One of the insurance companies lasted into the 1980s, but never grew like later competitors, Independent Life and American Heritage. Further, blacks lacked both the capital and opportunity to engage in major manufacturing ventures, wholesaling, railroading, and shipping. What resulted, as the survey in chapter 2 concluded, was growth in a small business economy that remained a shadow of its white counterpart.

When the recession came in 1914, black businesses lost ground. For young African-Americans, opportunity locally declined. Following the examples of Johnson, Waldron, Randolph, and others, they began to move North. World War I had reduced immigration and made jobs available. By 1916 the Pennsylvania Railroad and New York Central had begun recruiting black workers in Jacksonville. Iron and steel manufacturers sent recruiting agents offering six and seven dollars a day to people who worked for a dollar or less. Some, like Johnson, probably became part of the Renaissance in Harlem and other major cities.[60]

Initially the white community ignored the exodus, but as prosperity returned in 1916–17 and labor shortages appeared, Jacksonville's white business and political leaders confronted the situation. They asked black community leaders to discourage the migration, in part to protect their own businesses, which were losing workers. Black union leaders, however, challenged the advice, recognizing that labor shortages would benefit their wage prospects. From New York James Weldon Johnson voiced his approval of the migration. If Jacksonville businesses want to keep black workers, he wrote, they should pay decent wages, provide impartial treatment, and enforce laws fairly. The city council responded by passing legislation requiring recruiting agents to pay a $1,000 license fee; business leaders pressured the railroads to withdraw their recruiters; and local police harassed blacks attempting to board trains.[61]

The conflict reflected the dilemma of the New South. Jacksonville's African-American community had succeeded too well in encouraging a generation to work hard, seek opportunity, and advance themselves. When better jobs beckoned, they left their low-paying local employment. The white business community, locked into traditional racial and business doctrines, could not respond with better pay and conditions, but instead tried persuasion and then coercion to maintain control. The effort failed. The

James Weldon Johnson, principal of Stanton School, 1899–1903, novelist, diplomat, general secretary of the NAACP, composer with his brother of "Lift Every Voice and Sing." Courtesy of the Carpenter Library, University of North Florida.

Florida Times-Union saw no objection to black and white workers leaving town for better jobs. For Jacksonville, however, the loss of 6,000 enterprising young men and women hurt both the black community and the city for years to come.[62]

While there were many other voluntary associations in Jacksonville's black community, one needs special mention: the Republican party. From Reconstruction to the end of the nineteenth century, blacks voted Republican. In return, the party chose blacks to run as candidates in Jacksonville. As late as 1888, five blacks were city council members; attorney Joseph E. Lee served as municipal court judge; and the city employed black police and firefighters.[63]

The disfranchisement of Jacksonville voters in 1889, when the Democratic state legislature gave to the governor the power to appoint the city council and choose the mayor, ended Republican rule. Before Jacksonvillians regained the vote four years later, the legislature had passed the poll tax limiting voter participation, particularly for poor blacks. The Republican voter base was gone and the party did not regain power in the state until the 1960s. Meanwhile, in the city, white Democrats appealed to black voters in the primary elections during the 1890s. But after passage of the Democratic primary law in 1901 limiting that election to whites, blacks were excluded from any choice in the candidates who would be elected in this predominantly one-party state. Black voters predominated in the sixth ward and continued to elect representatives to the city council, until the state legislature gerrymandered ward boundaries in 1907 to exclude them. Thereafter, until the 1960s, blacks had no political power in local or state elections, except on referenda submitted to voters. Blacks still helped to nominate Republican presidential candidates and were rewarded, as Lee was with his appointment as Collector of Internal Revenue. That patronage ended, however, with the inauguration of the Democratic President, Woodrow Wilson, in 1913.[64]

As they lacked voting power and were restricted by the poll tax levy, it is not surprising that black voter registration declined after 1900. Statistics are incomplete, but 949 blacks were registered in 1906 (compared to 5,406 whites), and approximately 600 were registered in 1908 when black adults outnumbered whites in the city's population. Black political powerlessness in Jacksonville, as across the South, reflected a major component of the New South ideology. By whatever means necessary, white supremacy was the custom and law of the region.[65]

□ Clearly, the private sector played a major part in the growth and development of Jacksonville as a New South city. For inhabitants of this city, economic growth was important, but so, too, were good schools, parks and playgrounds, better health conditions, and community involvement. Businessmen, professionals, women, and minorities individually but more often through their voluntary associations cooperated with the public sector to make Jacksonville a modern city. Most of the efforts were modeled on national norms as Jacksonville sought to catch up with progressive programs in the nation.

There also were limitations. New South reforms were middle class. Labor unions and working-class people rarely were partners. Poor whites were "beneficiaries" in a *noblesse oblige* relationship. Whites saw blacks in the best of terms as junior partners. Blacks made the most of circumstances within a Jim Crow system. Middle-class white women made substantial breakthroughs leading to the ballot in 1919, though their achievements required male support in government or business, which meant men maintained ultimate control. Yet given these limitations, the participation of the voluntary associations became an essential component in the modernization of the New South city.

FIVE

Leisure Time and Leisure Values

In his book *City People: The Rise of Modern City Culture in Nineteenth-Century America*, historian Gunther Barth discusses the cultural changes taking place in American cities and their impact upon city people. The rise of urban institutions such as the apartment house, metropolitan newspaper, department store, ballpark, and vaudeville house helped immigrants of diverse backgrounds as well as rural American migrants to cities to begin to find a common ground of interests, life-styles, and values. The apartment house adapted "private space to a spatially divided city." The metropolitan press created a common language and communicated "pieces of urban identity." The department store encouraged a consumer role for women in city life and "made downtown the center of urban elegance." The ballpark gave meaning to "rules in the modern city" while helping to establish the place of spectators in popular culture. The vaudeville house "brought a sense of common humanity to diverse people" sharing cultural values with its audiences.[1]

In the New South cities, many of these same institutions had a similar impact, though sometimes delayed in time. For example, Jacksonville residents at the turn of the century already had a metropolitan newspaper, ballpark, and playhouse hosting vaudeville as well as legitimate theater. In the years following the fire, particularly among the middle class and the skilled working class, both white and black, the increasing availability of the five-and-one-half-day work week, holidays, and summer vacations provided more free time. In addition, a prospering economy afforded more discretionary spending money. As a result many residents began engaging in recreational activities similar to those in the cities to the North. New recreational opportunities in Jacksonville attracted entertainment seekers to the motion pictures, department store, and amusement park. Increasingly, the automobile as well as the streetcar and railroad provided greater access to resorts. Together they contributed to a popular if segregated culture shared by increasing numbers of Jacksonville residents. This distinctively urban culture also opened the doors to twentieth-century consumerism, the passive entertainment of spectators, and the pursuit of play as an alternative to the work ethic.[2]

Not all people, however, welcomed this new culture. Jacksonville, after all, was a city with roots in the antebellum South. Southern city dwellers, according to historian David R. Goldfield, had unique characteristics. They retained strong ties to the countryside: to land, farm, and nature. Many were recent migrants from rural areas. They had suspicions about cities and urban life. Their traditional values, coming from family, home, and church, did not automatically welcome cultural changes. Sometimes they felt city life threatened their religious beliefs and practices. It encouraged the freedom of individual choice at the expense of parental authority, a potential threat to family ties. While white southerners wanted the material prosperity that came with New South development, they were less sure about the accompanying cultural baggage. Above all, they were determined to maintain their special custom of racial superiority.[3]

Yet changes came to the New South cities, and Jacksonville was no exception. In this chapter I examine the developing popular culture and its impact on the community in the years after the Great Fire. I also look at some of the reactions to cultural change in people's efforts to maintain traditional family, religious, and cultural practices.

□ Among the most important local institutions for cultural change was the newspaper. The morning and Sunday *Florida Times-Union* and the evening *Metropolis* reported local news and events, linked readers with the outside world, encouraged support for Jacksonville's growth and prosperity, and tried to instruct readers in the white southern Democratic, generally conservative values of their publishers. The *Times-Union*, owned by the Florida East Coast Railroad, was the more influential of the papers, not only in Jacksonville but also across the state. Its circulation almost tripled in the fifteen years after the fire.[4]

Changes in newspaper format over the era broadened reader horizons. Special pages or sections devoted to finance, sports, women, automobiles, and local entertainment attracted readers. When the *Times-Union* encouraged attendance at baseball's opening day, or carnival's opening night, thousands responded. Both the women's pages and the automobile sections discussed the latest styles, bringing readers abreast of national trends. Newspaper advertising increased dramatically during the era for housing, furniture, clothing, household appliances, "Victrolas," and food. Sunday editions in the years immediately preceding the war so advertised the coming Christmas holidays as to suggest that the beginning of the "mass consumption" society may have occurred before the 1920s.[5]

For newcomers to Jacksonville, the newspapers provided information about jobs and housing. For tourists, there were notices of things to do. Young readers could learn about their city. Over the years the newspapers became the medium for choosing leisure activities. They advertised train schedules to the beaches, programs at vaudeville shows, movies, or amusement parks, sales at department stores, or the latest celebrity arriving in town. Citizen activists learned of public meetings, political rallies, or cultural performances. In effect, the newspapers communicated about Jacksonville, describing and helping to create the new urban culture.

They also communicated unevenly. Except for an occasional column entitled "News of Interest Among the Colored People," news of the African-American community was almost nonexistent. While the local press refrained from the excesses of William Randolph Hearst's yellow journalism, it also rarely achieved the professional standards of the "new journalism" developed during the late nineteenth century by Kansas City's William Rockhill Nelson or Joseph Pulitzer's *New York World*. Unlike the new journalism, local news columns carried opinion. Editorials shied away from exposing unsavory local conditions in order to improve them. Instead, a booster spirit too often purveyed half-truths about the city. Still, for white Jacksonvillians, the newspapers served to shape opinion, provide a common ground of knowledge, and open a window upon a modern culture to which many people aspired.[6]

A second major popular institution was the department store. Barth called it "the focal point for a novel form of downtown life. Its imposing appearance lent dignity to other, smaller shops that had gained a foothold among the wholesale establishments and warehouses, hotels and churches, banks and offices. Its alluring presentation of merchandise attracted legions of women." In New York, Chicago, and Philadelphia, A. T. Stewart, Marshall Field, and John Wanamaker, among others, set stan-

Savoy Theater. Reprinted from Caroline Rawls, comp., *Jacksonville Story*, 33.

dards of consumer opulence and, with the availability of limited credit, encouraged shopping as a popular pastime, leading toward a consumer society.[7]

For Jacksonville, the opening of Cohen Brothers' majestic department store in 1912 raised the city to new levels of urban sophistication. Prior to that time, the Cohens, Levy, Furchgott, and others had sold largely dry goods. In 1910, however, Morris Cohen hired Jacksonville's leading architect, Henry John Klutho, to design a new store that would occupy a full six-acre city block opposite Hemming Park. The resulting St. James Building dazzled Jacksonville. An estimated 28,000 people descended upon Cohen's for opening day. The building's main entrance opened onto the park. Its plate-glass windows were the first in Jacksonville. Inside, two orchestras played for shoppers and sightseers. A vast skylight flooded the interior of the department store with daylight. A fountain stood in the middle of the rotunda. A magnificent stairway invited people to a mezzanine supported in part by twenty-foot marble columns. Five hundred salespeople, live models wearing imported gowns, and a home furnishings department offering thousand-dollar Oriental carpets gave visitors a "big city impression." The *Times-Union* reported Cohen's to be the ninth largest department store in the nation and the largest for any city the size of Jacksonville.[8]

For shoppers, Cohen Brothers' presentation of European and American styles set standards for the local community. This new desire for sophistication also could be seen when a refurbished Levy Brothers' store opened and was advertised as "a Fifth Avenue shop set down in the center of Jacksonville" selling Hart, Schaffner and Marx suits. In addition to setting standards for style and creating an architectural ornament on the urban landscape, the department store encouraged consumerism. Women arrived by auto, streetcar, and cab to look, shop, and socialize, expanding their consumer role as part of the urban middle class. For Jacksonville, the department store anticipated the coming of the mid-twentieth-century shopping mall.[9]

A third cultural institution in American cities was the ballpark. Jacksonville's experience differed from the bigger northern cities in part because it hosted only a minor league baseball team. Rarely did the local South Atlantic League AA team draw large crowds. College football games were also occasional affairs, as when Florida played Georgia Tech or Stetson played Sewanee. Moncrief Park's race track lasted for only two years. Jacksonville lacked the urban spectator phenomenon, where fans escaped the congestion of the city streets, breathed deeply of fresh air at the park, and shared the excitement of major league competition. Also missing was the melting pot character of diverse classes, races, and ethnicities sharing a common experience. In biracial Jacksonville, black spectators sat in segregated bleachers down the left field line, and foreign-born residents comprised less than 5 percent of the population. Still, there were diverse classes; particularly noteworthy was the mixture of fans from both urban and rural backgrounds cheering together for their teams.[10]

When the major league teams came south for spring training in February, Jacksonville fans welcomed them warmly. Among the Brooklyn, Boston, Cincinnati, and Philadelphia teams that trained in Jacksonville during the era, Connie Mack's World Champion Athletics were the favorite. Even Rube Waddell, the A's star pitcher, "known for his intemperance and generally dissolute behavior," complained of too much hospitality from the locals who continually offered him food, drink, and other entertainment.[11]

Through the media, however, Jacksonville readers followed the exploits of big-league baseball, college football, horse and auto racing, golf, and prize fighting. When Jack Johnson kayoed Jim Jeffries to retain his heavyweight crown in 1910, black Jacksonvillians took to the streets to celebrate. Angry whites rioted in response. Again there were common bonds as well as racial antagonism.[12]

If spectator sports were only an occasional leisure-time activity, sports participation on sandlot, city, and high school baseball, football, and basketball teams provided young people with opportunities to hone their skills, learn teamwork, and play by the rules. At the turn of the century, the local National Guard or militia units fielded football teams that played on the college circuit. Later Duval High School athletes played Gainesville, Tampa, Lake City, Macon, and Savannah in three sports. A Duval High School girls' basketball team also played an interscholastic schedule. At Edward Waters College, Florida Baptist Academy, and Cookman Institute as well as on the sandlots, black athletes played baseball and football with one another, and against teams from out of town. A. Philip Randolph played first base and caught for the Cookman team.[13]

For participants and spectators, sports were an important leisure-time activity in the years before World War I. Historian Dale A. Somers suggests they served as a "social safety valve that allowed great masses of people to blow off steam in a relatively harmless way." As played, the games offered an outlet for the tension of urban life. They added excitement and glamour to peoples' lives. Jacksonville's smaller size and biracial character were limitations, however. The Sally League franchise was always a marginal operation, and the abolition of horse racing and Sunday sports during these years further restricted their impact upon the city's leisure culture.[14]

At the turn of the century, Jacksonville had one theater, which hosted vaudeville, plays, occasional operas, political celebrities, and a lyceum lecture series. It burned in the fire. Within a decade, however, at least eight new theaters offered movies, vaudeville, minstrel shows, and touring stock companies to local audiences. Perhaps most striking was the advent of the motion pictures. Begun with single-reelers in 1905, over the next decade films gradually replaced vaudeville at most theaters. Newspapers advertised the appearances of Mary Pickford, Lon Chaney, Lillian Gish, and John Barrymore. Moviegoers flocked to see D. W. Griffith's epic of white supremacy, *The Birth of a Nation*. They laughed with Oliver Hardy and Charlie Chaplin, ogled Theda Bara, and thrilled with the exploits of Douglas Fairbanks and William H. Hart. Ethel Barrymore, Sarah Bernhardt, and George M. Cohan came for personal appearances. Movie

Dixieland Amusement Park. Courtesy of the Haydon Burns Library.

patrons had many choices, as films stayed for only a day or two at local theaters. Black residents sat in segregated balconies, or went to their own theaters—the Globe, Palace, or Lincoln—to see movies or stage companies.[15]

In common with moviegoers across the nation, Jacksonville fans became part of an urban and national culture of film fantasy and star gazing, enjoying the escape to action, comedy, and romance. Yet there was more. "Overwhelmingly," Robert Sklar has written, "films of contemporary life, crime movies, melodramas and love stories centered on men and women from the upper-middle and wealthy classes: people who lived in large spacious houses, kept servants, owned cars and earned their money from business, finance or the professions." Americans admired their material splendor. They fantasized with their film romances. They identified with the lawmen who violently subdued criminals. For young people and country folk new to city ways, movies offered values distinctly different from those of an older America, and they became a "major factor in the reorientation of traditional values."[16]

A more sinister impact of the new motion pictures could be seen in the 1915 production of *The Birth of a Nation*, a film that historian Joel Williamson compares with *Gone With the Wind* in its regional and national popularity. Where *Gone With the Wind*'s romantic portrayal of the Lost

Cause generally had a benign effect upon moviegoers, *Birth of a Nation* had a divisive impact, blaming African-Americans for causing the Civil War and for undermining the Reconstruction by "reversion to bestiality." According to Thomas W. Dixon, Jr., the author of *The Clansman* from which the film was adapted, it required the heroic efforts of white southerners to restore peace and harmony to the region in the form of white supremacy. This popularization of the Reconstruction myth for millions of viewers across the country helped shape racial attitudes nationally and reinforce Jim Crow practices in Jacksonville and across the South.[17]

Film and vaudeville were not the only entertainments helping to create a biracial popular culture in Jacksonville during these years. The expansion of amusement parks and the opening of the beaches also helped encourage a leisure ethic as an alternative to work. Jacksonville's first amusement park was the Ostrich Farm, located out Talleyrand Avenue in the Fairfield section east of downtown. It opened in the winter of 1898–99. Initially visitors, mostly tourists, could watch ostriches race, ride in ostrich-drawn carts, or even saddle up one of the big birds. Over the years, as the result of competition with newer amusement parks, the entertainment concept expanded. The Ostrich Farm moved to larger park sites, adding alligators, baby lions, pumas, leopards, sloths, and other jungle animals, and becoming the Ostrich Farm and Zoo. By 1907 visitors could see lion wrestling, balloons ascending with parachute jumps, performing stallions, comedy acrobats, high-wire acts, and free vaudeville. They could ride roller coasters or merry-go-rounds and frequent the dance hall, bathing beach, ice cream parlor, or band concerts. Tickets cost ten cents, later increasing to twenty-five cents per person.[18]

Competing with the Ostrich Farm was Phoenix Park, begun by the Jacksonville Street Railways on the suburban fringe of Springfield northeast of downtown to encourage Sunday utilization of the city's streetcar lines by local residents. In 1907 Dixieland Amusement Park opened across the St. Johns River in South Jacksonville, a ferryboat ride from downtown. The *Times-Union* called Dixieland "The Coney Island of the South." The park contained thirty acres with 100,000 feet of river frontage. In addition to a 1,600-seat theater, there was a Figure-Eight ride, toboggan, merry-go-round, dance pavilion, electric fountain, curio shop, swimming area in the St. Johns River (and later a hundred-foot pool), commons for baseball or circuses (and later a ballpark for the Jacksonville Sally League team), refreshment pavilion, dog and pony show, photographic gallery, laughing gallery, circle swing, "House of Troubles," botanical garden, and animal life exhibit. A major fire destroyed a large segment of Dixieland in 1909; it was rebuilt but suffered another fire a year later; and finally was closed. In 1916 the Southland Amusement Park opened on the site and the Ostrich Farm relocated nearby. For the black community on the northwest edge of the city, the streetcar company opened Lincoln Park in 1903. A short-lived Mason Park also provided leisure-time entertainment. Though amusements at both parks were of lesser quality, there were band concerts, dance pavilions, a merry-go-round, baseball games, roller coasters, food concessions, and vaudeville shows.[19]

For both black and white Jacksonville, for young people and newcomers to the city, the amusement park offered excitement. It encouraged extravagance, gaiety, abandon, and revelry, challenging the traditional values of thrift, sobriety, hard work, and ambition. As John F. Kasson has written, the amusement park "broke down the sense of rigidity that dominated so much of the life of American cities at the turn of the century." Its informality led to conviviality and the sharing of experiences among different peoples. The amusement park "signaled the rise of a new mass culture no longer deferential to genteel tastes and values." Temporarily it served as a spectacular, exotic, "liberated social setting," compared with the disciplines of daily life.[20]

Another alternative for Jacksonville residents during this era was the beaches. Henry Flagler's Florida East Coast Railroad rebuilt the branch line to Pablo (now Jacksonville) Beach in 1900, and his Florida East Coast Hotel system opened the Continental Hotel at Atlantic Beach that June. The *Times-Union* called the hotel "the South's most elegant summer resort" and a fitting addition to Flagler's holdings in St. Augustine, Palm Beach, and down state.[21]

The Continental became a first-class resort, drawing vacationers from Florida, Georgia, Alabama, and the Carolinas as well as the more affluent people of Jacksonville. Over the years it changed owners and its name to the Atlantic Hotel. It also opened a golf course, trap shoot, and tennis courts at the beach and became a convention center. On Independence Day, the hotel staged extravaganzas of golf and tennis tournaments, military drills, auto and motorcycle races on the beach, field sports, dances, and cabaret entertainment capped with fireworks. The *Times-Union* called it the "veritable Atlantic City of the South."[22]

More popular and less expensive were the facilities at Pablo Beach, known as the "playground of Jacksonville." Weekend vacationers chose from eight trains daily to get there from South Jacksonville. Once at the beach, they could rent house tents "with floors and screens," flats, cottages, bungalows, take rooms at the Ocean View Hotel, or return home that night. For entertainment, they could rent a car or bicycle, buy snacks, ice cream and meals from various beach emporia, dance at the Budweiser Hoffbrau, enjoy a cabaret at the East Coast Inn, or even venture to Palmetto Lodge, Cora Taylor Crane's seaside annex to her brothel in town. The Pablo Beach Fourth of July featured parades, racing, sports, dancing, and fireworks. Thousands came on summer weekends by train or, after the completion of Atlantic Boulevard in 1910, by car.[23]

Farther north between Atlantic Beach and the village of Mayport along the coast, blacks went to segregated Manhattan Beach. Opening in 1907, it offered cottages, a restaurant, dance pavilion, and bath houses for adults, and a merry-go-round, swings, and other amusements for children. It became a favorite spot for summer excursions by black churches and their parishioners.[24]

The beach experience was more than an escape from the city, though the ocean breezes surely made summer weekends more bearable than in town. Weekend house parties, church outings, and family holidays strengthened social bonds in a relaxing environment. Golf, tennis, boardwalk, and surf accentuated the alternatives to work and encouraged an early stage of the play ethic that over the years has increasingly influenced the lives of middle- and working class Americans.

For Jacksonville residents and visitors, the opportunities to use leisure time in new ways grew in the years before World War I. Traditional activities in the home or church continued, but the newer outlets of shopping, or going to the movie theater, ballpark, amusement park, or beaches brought changes to the lives of city residents. In the process, a newer urban culture with its opportunities for consumption or play challenged traditional religious values about the primacy of work, thrift, or self-control and changed in part the character of this New South city.

These changes came partly from the era's economic prosperity and the encouragement of business, government, and the media. The enterprising businessmen of the era built and operated department stores, amusement parks, beach hotels, and movie houses. Local government supported these efforts with crowd control, police and fire protection, and personal endorsement of special events. Improved transportation also provided better access to places of entertainment. The era's prosperity until 1914 produced a higher standard of living, more free time, and more discretionary income. Improved communications, especially in the press, helped generate enthusiasm. Finally, Jacksonville's rapid population growth created markets for leisure entrepreneurs.[25]

For city dwellers, leisure activities provided an escape from the rigors of daily life, a change of pace, before returning to work. People sought the social liberation of park, oceanfront, theater, or department store. Sharing a special holiday at the beach, a film at the movies, or a Sunday at Dixieland Park gave them a sense of personal freedom to choose play over work or other obligations. In Jacksonville, people wanted to become part of mainstream America: to hear Theodore Roosevelt, William Jennings Bryan, Eugene Debs, Jacob Riis, Alice Paul, or Woodrow Wilson speak in person, enjoy Sarah Bernhardt or Ethel Barrymore on stage, attend concerts by Walter Damrosch and the New York Symphony, or watch Ty Cobb, Nap Rucker, or Connie Mack in spring training. People sensed that Jacksonville was becoming a city with a popular culture less provincial and more urbane. The media reflected this change repeatedly. The increasing variety of leisure activities contributed to greater individual freedom and this New South city coming of age.

□ The changing character of Jacksonville's popular culture, however, did not completely overshadow traditional community values and mores. In fact, most residents probably continued favorite pastimes and activities, some ignoring the innovations, others adapting and enjoying both the old and the new. For traditional leisure activities, North Florida's climate played a major role. Residents hunted in winter and fished the St. Johns River and its many tributaries in warmer weather. Summer's intense heat and humidity slowed the pace of life. Affluent residents escaped to the North Carolina mountains or beyond for relief. Less fortunate local children cooled themselves, playing or swimming in the many rivers or creeks. Their parents and grandparents sipped iced beverages, fanned themselves with palm leaves, and rocked on front porches, perhaps visiting with family, friends, or neighbors. School opened later in the fall and closed earlier in the spring, in part due to the heat. The theater, vaudeville, and motion picture season began in October and lasted through May. Mild winters enabled country club members to enjoy their golf and tennis and yacht clubbers their boats almost year round. River excursions also were available most of the year for church groups and others, though they became more popular in the warmer months. Meanwhile less reputable activities in the saloons, pool halls, brothels, and opium dens attracted their customers and provided an escape from both the heat and the cold throughout the year. Following one of his trips to Jacksonville, Baltimore humorist H. L. Mencken claimed, probably tongue-in-cheek, that they made the city "a metropolis comparable to Ninevah and Gomorrah in their prime, with the hottest night-clubs between Norfolk and Miami."[26]

Pablo Beach. Courtesy of the Haydon Burns Library.

Yet of all the leisure-time activities, probably none attracted more participation from both blacks and whites, and especially from women, than Jacksonville's churches and synagogues. Jacksonville, like most southern and other American communities at the turn of the century, had strong religious traditions. Christian worshippers attended religious services Sunday mornings and evenings, and often on Wednesday nights. Jews observed their Sabbaths on Friday nights and Saturdays. Young people had their special groups, men their fellowships, such as the Protestant Episcopal Church Club, and women their leagues, associations, or circles. There also was a YMCA, YWCA, and YMHA as well as scout troops often affiliated with church or synagogue. The churches had their pot-luck suppers, choirs, concerts, and revivals. They raised money from bazaars and rummage sales for foreign missions or to help the poor. They observed the religious holidays as well as such secular holidays as Thanksgiving. Black churches also celebrated Emancipation Day and Frederick Douglass's birthday. A 1906 survey of Jacksonville's churches and synagogues estimated 8,400 white Christian and Jewish members in a city population of 15,000 whites. (African-Americans were not included in the survey.) Reflecting the social stratification of the white community, Episcopalians (1,400) and Presbyterians (680) together comprised about one-fourth of the total. Methodists were the largest single adult denomination (1,850) followed by the Christian churches or Disciples of Christ

(950), and Baptists (760). Roman Catholics numbered 2,000, including approximately 800 adults. There were 400 Lutherans and 75 Christian Scientists. Half the 150 Jews belonged to the Orthodox synagogue and half to the Reformed temple, Ahavath Chesed. The number of white churches and synagogues more than doubled during the fifteen years after the fire (from twenty-four to fifty-five and one to two), but were still fewer than the seventy-seven black churches.[27]

Baptist, Methodist, Lutheran, Congregational, Disciples, and Presbyterian churches sponsored revivals frequently throughout the era. In 1905 the Union Revival Association, comprising most of the black and white Protestant denominations in the city, organized a mammoth six-week revival. The local newspapers never reported why this major effort was required, but clearly religious leaders saw something amiss in the growing commercialization and secularization of this New South city after the fire. A 6,500-seat tabernacle was built especially for the occasion across from Hemming Park. An estimated 6,000 people heard the Reverend Dr. L. W. Munhall preach what the *Times-Union* called "the greatest sermon ever heard in Jacksonville . . . to the greatest congregation ever assembled in the city. . . . [for] the greatest revival Jacksonville has ever had." The extent to which the sermon and revival revitalized the faithful, recaptured the backsliders, or converted the unregenerate souls remains unknown.[28]

Church people also voiced their concern about what they considered to be social evils or vices (though rarely about the increasing racial segregation). This concern, according to historian Ted Ownby, came out of a deeply felt evangelical Protestant faith that focused on family, home, and church, and feared the incursion of secular activities, especially on the Sabbath, which might weaken or subvert one's faith or morals. This fear was particularly true regarding commercial activities, such as sporting games, vaudeville, amusement parks, and films over which religious leaders heretofore had little control.[29]

Concerns about commercial amusements on the Sabbath were ongoing. A ministerial meeting in March 1903 condemned Sunday bicycle racing at the recently opened Bicycle Coliseum. The following year the city's leading Presbyterian minister and head of the Ministerial Association proposed an ordinance to ban Sunday bicycle racing, baseball, horse racing, and other commercial amusements. While it failed to pass, the state legislature enacted a law in 1905 to ban Sunday baseball, football, bowling, and horse racing. Responding to these pressures, Jacksonville mayors enforced the Sunday blue laws, not only for commercial sports but

The ostrich farm. Courtesy of Wayne W. Wood.

in saloons and grocery, dry goods, and shoe stores. Restaurants, hotels, and boardinghouses could serve food on Sundays but not liquor. Shops selling newspapers, cigars, ice cream, milk, and prescription medicines remained open.[30]

In 1909 the Jacksonville Ministerial Alliance, supported by the Woman's Club, persuaded the city council to close all theaters and other places of amusements on Sunday. The owners of the Ostrich Farm responded by threatening to shut down the city's premiere tourist attraction. Theater owners successfully obtained an injunction to block the ordinance, but in 1912 the city council passed another law with strong ministerial support banning Sunday vaudeville, circuses, carnivals, plays, minstrel shows, and street parades. Only the motion pictures were exempt. Yet they were subject to censorship by the Woman's Club and closed during Sunday evening church services.[31]

The effect of the Sunday blue laws on Jacksonville's growth and development as a New South city is impossible to measure. Probably it was negligible. Other southern cities had similar ordinances, and even in the Northeast, some city governments banned commercial sports and other Sunday activities. Locally, most businessmen and professionals, many of whom were also church lay leaders, probably accepted six days for business and piety on the Sabbath. At least the men still could purchase their Sunday paper and cigars. For working men and women laboring five-and-one-half-day weeks, some probably felt their leisure time was unnecessarily restricted. Yet others, faithful to their evangelical Protestant religious traditions, undoubtedly supported them, as did most of the clergy. The Sunday closings reflected their still-strong commitment to the commandment to keep the Sabbath holy. It also may have reflected their concerns to maintain church attendance in the face of increasing and attractive commercial competition.

Another area of concern was gambling. In 1909 Moncrief track opened for a winter season of horse racing. Shortly thereafter the *Florida Times-Union* reported substantial gambling on the premises. One downstate newspaper asked why Jacksonville police arrested blacks for playing the numbers but not whites betting on horses. Subsequently the Church Club, a Protestant Episcopal lay group open to all white Protestants, attacked horse racing as a major barrier to civic progress in Jacksonville. It brought a wrong class of people to the city, they said, corrupting morals and destroying business. That night club members formed an antiracing league to abolish the track. The next two months saw spirited action both for and against horse racing in both Jacksonville and Tallahassee. References to its prohibition in St. Louis, New Orleans, and New York were cited. Supporters of the track argued that Pinkertons guarded the park to exclude minors and no liquor was sold on the grounds. In May, however, the legislature banned the sport with but one opposing vote. The Ministerial Alliance expressed its gratitude. A week later the Jacksonville track burned. The *Times-Union* suspected arson.[32]

Meanwhile, Jacksonville's church people and reformers became concerned about the city's red-light district. Like many municipalities across the United States, Jacksonville geographically segregated its brothels largely to the predominantly black neighborhood of LaVilla. The most prominent house belonged to Cora Taylor Crane, widow of poet and novelist Stephen Crane. Her handsome house, "The Court," opened in 1900

Jacksonville's resort hotel, first known as the Continental and then as the Atlantic Hotel, which opened in 1901 and burned in 1919. Courtesy of Wayne W. Wood.

and employed thirteen "regulars," mostly white girls from poor families in the hinterlands of Florida, south Georgia, and eastern Alabama. Crane also owned Palmetto Lodge, her annex at Pablo Beach. Early in the twentieth century, black church leaders had criticized the brothels as disruptive to the welfare of the black community. But most whites appeared to accept them as a necessary evil in a commercial, seaport, tourist town. Carrie Nation came to Jacksonville in 1908, challenging the existence of both the saloons and brothels. She visited three of the houses and spoke with the girls, "who were clearly impressed by what she had to say." Still, no action was taken.[33]

In 1912 the organization of a Men and Religion Forward Movement by fourteen Protestant congregations challenged Jacksonville's middle-class Christians to become involved in social and economic problems, including child labor, poverty, juvenile justice, and prostitution. That September, Jesse Bowman Young, the departing reform-minded minister from Snyder Memorial Methodist Church, gave a major address under the auspices of the Ministerial Association on "the social evil" and praised the efforts of northern cities to eliminate prostitution as part of a larger program of progressive reform. Jacksonville's mayor, William Jordan, promised to look into the problem. His successor, Van C. Swearingen, went further, making the abolition of prostitution a major part of his administration. He supported the reformers when they opened Bethesda Mission to help "fallen women" in the spring of 1914. He also endorsed the Ministerial Alliance and the Woman's Interdenominational Rescue Movement's call to close all brothels. At the same time, however, Swearingen also voiced concern about what the prostitutes would then do. In response, 285 Riverside Presbyterian Church members pledged to help as many of the ladies as would accept it. Dr. J. Lindsay Patton, rector of the Protestant Episcopal Church of the Good Shepherd, offered to take several of them into his home and treat them as family. Swearingen gave the executive order to close down the red-light district and the women scattered, some to other parts of Jacksonville and others outside the city. For a brief period, the campaign against prostitution succeeded in closing the city's brothels and driving the practice underground. The success, however, was temporary. By the end of the era, under a different mayoral administration, prostitution had returned to LaVilla.[34]

The final major concern for Jacksonville's moral reformers was prohibition. Nationally, the campaign to prohibit the manufacture and sale of alcoholic beverages had political, social, economic, and moral ramifications. Women and children particularly were victims of alcoholic abuse. The liquor lobby, from corner saloon to brewer and distiller, influenced local and state politics. Work force accidents due to drinking were costly for both employers and employees. In addition, evangelical Protestantism strongly opposed drinking as immoral since early in the nineteenth century. All of these factors made the issue important, and Jacksonville, like many American cities after the turn of the century, had chapters of both the Women's Christian Temperance Union (WCTU) and the Anti-Saloon League.

In the early years after the fire, the emphasis locally was on temperance. However, when the Georgia legislature passed its prohibition amendment in 1907, pressures for a similar action increased locally. Moderates in city government tried to hold off more radical changes by strengthening existing laws to regulate and restrict local saloons. The city council raised liquor license fees to drive out of business smaller, presumably less respectable bars. The mayor cracked down on illegal sales in dives and brothels. Saloons were racially segregated so no black musicians could play in resorts frequented by whites, and no whites could drink in establishments owned and patronized by blacks. City attorney John Barrs believed that unless dives were eliminated and decent saloons segregated, citizens of Duval County might support a prohibition referendum.[35]

Despite the city's efforts to control liquor sales, local dry leaders continued to push for total prohibition. In the fall of 1907 they sponsored a series of rallies to obtain petition signatures for a prohibition referendum. Banker, progressive, and U.S. senatorial candidate John N. C. Stockton supported them, as did the clergy, conservative congressman Frank Clark, and business leaders like W. W. Cummer. Businessmen formed both prohibition and antiprohibition groups depending on their commercial interests, ethnic backgrounds, or religious beliefs. Despite their efforts, the petitioners failed to make the ballot for a special spring election. Locally, county commissioners claimed there were an insufficient number of valid signatures. Too many were duplicates or unregistered voters.[36]

The following February, Carrie Nation made her four-day visit to Jacksonville, speaking at Bethel Baptist Institutional Church, Ebeneezer Methodist Episcopal Church, First Christian Church, and the Ostrich Farm, culminating with a big Women's Christian Temperance Union rally. She also toured several saloons and brothels. Despite threatening weather at the Ostrich Farm, more than 1,000 people heard her attack whiskey, tobacco, and the pictures of nude women hanging over the bars in local saloons. She criticized men for their bad habits and attitudes. One reporter later admitted her observations were "pretty close to the mark."[37]

Meanwhile the prohibition campaign continued across the state. When the legislature convened for its biennial session in 1909, the reformers were ready. On April 24 the lawmakers passed their amendment to the state constitution that would go before the voters in a referendum in November 1910. That fall the Anti-Saloon League led the campaign against the estimated 330 saloons statewide (about one-third of them in Jacksonville or Duval County), the liquor interests, and the "big city newspapers." Prohibitionists organized, rallied, and prayed for victory. On November 8 the WCTU sponsored a parade of 1,000 schoolchildren, 300 women, and 100 men to Hemming Park. Bands played and white Protestant church people from every city neighborhood took part. Yet the local vote was clearly wet. In the election the following week, every ward went against the amendment, and the city-county vote together came within one hundred of providing the statewide majority. Ironically, Jacksonville's African-American church leaders might have helped prohibition to succeed, but the *Times-Union* estimated that only about 200 voted due to poll taxes, racist arguments against drinking, and exclusionary policies practiced by the dominant white Democratic majority.[38]

Subsequently the city council passed further liquor legislation licensing dealers, setting hours, restricting locations (an early form of zoning),

Klutho's film studios, one of many in Jacksonville, owned by architect H.J. Klutho. Reprinted from Caroline Rawls, comp., *The Jacksonville Story*, 82.

barring women from saloons (they could drink in restaurants and hotels), prohibiting minors, drunkards, and lewd paintings, and continuing racial segregation. At each session thereafter, Florida's legislature attempted to enact prohibition. In 1915 it passed bills closing bars at 6:00 P.M., restricting sales of food with alcoholic beverages, barring liquor by the drink (half pints and larger were available), and forbidding women and minors from working in wholesale or mail-order liquor establishments. These laws had little effect in Jacksonville, however; critics charged that Mayor Bowden was not interested in their enforcement. Following the election of Governor Sidney J. Catts in 1916, a one-time Baptist preacher and strong prohibitionist, the legislature again enacted a constitutional amendment to come before the voters in November 1918.[39]

Until the nation's entry into World War I, a majority of Jacksonville and Duval County residents held firm in their opposition to prohibition. As in Baltimore, New Orleans, and other cities across the region and nation, there were enough Catholics, Jews, German Lutherans, and sometimes Episcopalians as well as merchant mariners, hotelkeepers, restauranteurs, and other business people oriented toward trade or tourism, in Jacksonville to block this white evangelical Protestant reform. As a result, Duval became one of only two counties in Florida to remain wet.

The Jacksonville religious community did not limit its reform interests to moralistic issues. Prohibition, of course, had social, economic, and political ramifications for the family, workplace, and voting booth. A Presbyterian minister was a prime mover in organizing the Children's Home Society of Florida in Jacksonville in 1901. The Ministerial Alliance locally initiated the movement for the five-and-one-half-day workweek. It also established the Rescue Mission as a home for "fallen women." Jacksonville clergy helped in the formation of Associated Charities and in its reopening following the recession of 1914. They supported better schools, new hospitals, child labor reform, and better community health care. The Ministerial Association even endorsed candidates, supporting Stockton in the U.S. senatorial primary of 1908.[40]

Religious support for social action locally had a broad base. Episcopalians and Presbyterians frequently took the lead, but Methodists, Baptists, Disciples, Congregationalists, and Lutherans joined with them. The reform rabbis also played a role. This activism involved both clergy and laypeople. While the ministers frequently worked through their Ministerial Association, lay men and women such as Ada, Ninah, and Waldo Cummer, Lina Barnett, attorney Richard P. Daniel, lumber merchant George Drew, and banker George DeSaussure spoke through the YMCA, YWCA, Church Club, and the Men and Religion Forward Movement.

Clearly Jacksonville churches and synagogues offered the community more than simply sacraments, ceremonies, and rites from baptism, christening, or bris, through marriage to the grave. They also provided opportunity for a variety of leisure-time activities. They contributed to the character of Jacksonville's popular culture. Even more important, they asserted community values based on their teachings in a changing urban society. At the same time, and perhaps fortunately, their powers were also limited, as seen in the failure to achieve prohibition. A later generation might view many of those moralistic reforms with legitimate skepticism, but Progressive Era Jacksonvillians expressed their form of the Social Gospel as part of the New South quest for economic and civic progress.[41]

In the end, Jacksonville's transition to a modern, New South city brought changes in its popular culture, challenges to traditional values, and conflicts between advocates of the old and new. Many of the issues were never totally resolved. In subsequent years, the advent of radio, television, and other culture technologies would accelerate those changes, producing further conflicts in community values. Eventually traditional values would give ground in Sunday commerce, gambling, prohibition, and even white supremacy, though not without a fight. Changes also took place with an increasing consumerism challenging habits of saving and frugality; more play time competing with a traditional work ethic; and an increased spectator role in leisure activities suggesting a more passive approach to life. In many cases, greater individual freedom came at the expense of family, church, work, or community responsibilities. Thus, changes taking place in Jacksonville and other cities in the Progressive Era became part of what, for good or for ill, has continued across the region and country throughout the twentieth century.

SIX

World War I Comes to Jacksonville

The European war beginning in 1914 already had significantly hurt Jacksonville's economy. Due to embargoes, the transatlantic export of pine, nitrates, and naval stores fell sharply, reverberating throughout the city's financial community. Construction declined while many shops, offices, and several thousand houses stood vacant. A second major impact was the departure of an estimated 6,000 African-Americans beginning in 1915 to work in northern industry. Still, local groups reached out to victims of war. Club women and the growing Middle Eastern, primarily Lebanese, community aided Syrian refugees. Others "adopted" French children, sending clothing and medical supplies to war-ravaged villages.[1]

National preparedness also had its repercussions locally. In March 1917 Mayor J. E. T. Bowden named a local preparedness committee, called a mass meeting to support universal military training, and urged Jacksonville residents to display the American flag. Merrill-Stevens Company, Jacksonville's largest shipbuilder, began to expand its facilities to construct more and larger merchant vessels.[2]

Following the congressional declaration of war on April 6, thousands of Jacksonville residents gathered in Hemming Park to support the decision. The local naval militia unit was mobilized, and the National Guard called for volunteers. Within a week young patriots had formed an infantry battalion. Older residents, meanwhile, organized a Home Guard to maintain order for local emergencies. Meanwhile black community leaders petitioned the governor for their own military unit. Club women concerned about food supplies began finding vacant lots for planting vegetable gardens. German-Americans, aware of their possible identification with the enemy, offered their Germania Club building on Riverside Avenue for Red Cross emergency use and adopted resolutions of loyalty to the United States. At the end of April African-Americans rallied in a massive parade and demonstration in Oakland Park. An estimated 25,000 blacks heard Mayor Bowden and School Superintendent Fons A. Hathaway, along with President John A. Gregg of Edward Waters College, attorney Joseph E. Lee, developer Joseph Blodgett, and Abraham Lincoln Lewis of the Afro-American Insurance Company rally black business, labor, fraternal, and religious groups in support of the war effort. Across town, Jacksonville business leaders through the Real Estate Exchange and Chamber of Commerce began lobbying for a military camp at Black Point, on the St. Johns River, eight miles southwest of downtown.[3]

That spring Jacksonville also held a mayor-council election to replace Bowden, who was considered too accommodating of the infant movie industry's excesses and lax in enforcing laws against brothels and liquor by the drink. His successor was John W. Martin, a popular young salesman favored by reform-minded Democrats. Meanwhile in Tallahassee, the state legislature in its biennial session passed a constitutional amendment for prohibition and legislation to replace Jacksonville's mayor–council–Board of Trustees system of city government with a city commission. Jacksonville state senator Ion L. Farris also secured authorization for a bond referendum to build the first automobile bridge across the St. Johns River, later ratified by Jacksonville voters. When the new city commission met that summer, it appointed the first women to serve in government, on the boards of charities and recreation. Progressive reform appeared to have peaked.[4]

That June Jacksonville business and political leaders intensified their efforts to obtain a military camp at Black Point. A year earlier United States Senator Duncan U. Fletcher had written Secretary of War Newton D. Baker to consider using Black Point as a base for mobilizing troops to punish Pancho Villa for his geurilla raids across the Texas border from Mexico. No action was taken then, but following American entry into World War I, the tempo picked up. Fletcher and Jacksonville congressman William J. Sears wrote Secretary Baker, who directed General Leonard Wood to investigate conditions at Black Point. An aide initially reported back after a rainy day's inspection about mosquitoes, malaria, and marshland. A subsequent visit by Wood on a clear, sunny day brought a positive response. Yet in July Baker wrote Fletcher bypassing Jacksonville for sites in Mississippi and Louisiana, claiming "military strategic reasons." Fletcher continued to lobby for Jacksonville, and when a decision was made to establish a quartermasters' training camp, Baker approved the creation of Camp Joseph E. Johnston at Black Point. Construction began in October and the first trainees arrived on November 19, 1917. The congressional delegation, supported by the Chamber of Commerce and local business groups, had achieved its goal.[5]

Before the first troops arrived, however, federal officials came to Jacksonville to warn the mayor and sheriff to clamp a tight lid on vice before the opening of the camp. Earlier, Secretary Baker had written to all of the state governors and state councils of defense about his concern for the "youth of the country [who] will be gathered together for a period of intensive discipline and training. The greater proportion of this force," he wrote, "probably will be made up of young men who have not yet become accustomed to contact with either the saloon or the prostitute." It was important to safeguard them "against temptation to which they are not accustomed." President Wilson already had signed legislation authorizing the War Department to suppress prostitution and prohibit the sale of alcohol to any member of the military while in uniform. Cities and towns, Baker concluded, must assume responsibility for clean conditions.[6]

Conditions in Jacksonville were far from clean. Following Mayor Van Swearingen's efforts to suppress prostitution in 1914, his successor, Bowden, had relaxed enforcement efforts and the LaVilla red-light district had reopened. Now Martin, his successor, promised to cooperate with the War Department, but May Jennings, president of the Florida Federation of Women's Clubs, was skeptical. In October she wrote Raymond B. Fosdick, chairman of the War Department's Commission on Training Camp Activities in Washington, to complain about Camp Johnston's new commanding officer, who had been quoted in the newspapers as not too concerned about Jacksonville's wetness as long as alcohol was not sold to men in uniform.[7]

Her fears were reinforced the following January when Frank L. Mulholland, president of Rotary International, arrived in town on a tour of training camps in the South. In a speech to the local Rotary, he reported there were more drunken soldiers on the streets of Jacksonville the preceding Saturday night than he had ever seen in any other city. In addition, certain hotels permitted both prostitution and drinking. Meanwhile at Camp Johnston, Lieutenant Colonel Fred L. Munson, the command-

Merrill-Stevens Shipyards. Courtesy of the Haydon Burns Library.

ing officer, had a change of heart. Where Jacksonville's wetness had been no problem for him in October, he now endorsed prohibition, announcing that "the selling of whiskey in Jacksonville has proven detrimental to the soldiers." A month later in a letter to the president of the Chamber of Commerce, Munson warned that unless Duval County held and ratified a referendum prohibiting the sale of alcoholic beverages, he would restrict his officers and men to the base, except on Sundays.[8]

At the chamber, the Board of Governors unanimously endorsed prohibition as a patriotic measure to protect the troops. "Liquor is a bad thing for a soldier," said one governor, and we must get on with "the main business of the nation at this time [which] is the making of a victorious army." The chamber established a special Committee of Fifteen under the direction of developer Telfair Stockton to mobilize community opinion and secure a countywide referendum. By March a petition signed by one-quarter of the voters endorsed the referendum, and the county commissioners called for a May election. Strong support for the chamber on the referendum came from the Jacksonville Ministerial Alliance and the Woman's Club, long advocates of prohibition. Hotel men and liquor dealers formed a Fair Play Association to rally the wets. That spring both sides staged parades and demonstrations, advertising their views in the daily press. The drys, however, had the edge, linking prohibition to patriotism, and in the referendum on May 14, they outvoted the wets. In Jacksonville a surprising 80 percent of the registered voters went to the polls, returning a dry majority of 2,384 to 1,865. The state prohibition amendment passed by the legislation the preceding spring also passed in Jacksonville the following November.[9]

Clearly, prohibition came to Jacksonville as a patriotic measure, and the Chamber of Commerce support was crucial. Before, in 1910, the chamber did not take sides, and Jacksonville voters defeated prohibition. In 1907 prohibitionists could not even get the issue on the ballot. This time the chamber endorsement, when added to the traditional support of middle-class white and black women and the evangelical Protestant religious community, provided the margin for a dry victory. The victory, however, was not total. Nassau County to the north still sold liquor freely at least until November 1918, and the illegal sale of whiskey and sexual favors in Jacksonville continued throughout the war.[10]

□ An issue affecting almost all Jacksonville residents as well as other Americans during the war was the supply of food. As early as May 1917 the *Florida Times-Union* reported shortages. Mayor Bowden urged local residents not to waste food. Anticipating the harvesting of vegetables from the vacant-lot gardens, club women introduced canning lessons in the Mothers Clubs. Meanwhile the local chapter of the National Negro Business League sponsored canning demonstrations for 200 black farmers and gardeners at Bethel Baptist Institutional Church.[11]

That fall agents from the National Food Administration came to Jacksonville to plan a food conservation campaign. Local clergy responded by preaching sermons in support. The newspapers printed pledge cards for food conservation, which 16,500 families signed. Two major downtown hotels started "meatless Tuesdays," in which no meat in any form was served that day. Next, wheat breads were eliminated on Wednesdays. The practice spread across the city into homes and boardinghouses. In December fuel shortages prompted authorities to proclaim two lightless nights per week. By January 1918 local businesses were forgoing heat one day per week to save coal. Fortunately, the first "coalless" day was a mild one.[12]

Beginning in June 1917, Jacksonville residents also began subscribing to the first of the Liberty Loan drives. The whole community seemed to join in support. Boy Scouts passed out literature on street corners explaining the campaign. Civic clubs and club women added their support and pledges. Kicking off the third Liberty Loan in April 1918 were a pageant and a parade, in which 10,000 to 12,000 people marched, including 5,000 African-Americans. Participating were both black and white bands, church groups, fraternal orders, and workers from the shipyards and mills, though on a segregated basis. At the request of the Federal Reserve Board, the city council postponed further public improvements for the duration of the war, pledging instead $120,000 to the campaign. The Afro-American Insurance Company bought $10,000 of liberty bonds. In the July Liberty Loan drive, the *Florida Times-Union* editors sensed the strong biracial support for the war effort as the crowds cheered black as well as white units marching in the parade. An editorial praised both Jacksonville's blacks and its handful of Chinese residents for participating, noting that "the negroes [*sic*] of this country are doing their duty as Americans as well as the white men of the land."[13]

With the arrival of the trainees at Camp Johnston in November 1917, Jacksonvillians organized a local Commission on Training Camp Activities to provide suitable entertainment for soldiers on weekend passes into town. They also invited convalescing soldiers for meals and entertainment in private homes. The *Florida Times-Union* began a campaign that had 3,227 trainees invited for family Christmas dinners. Meanwhile Congregation Ahavath Chesed provided a special reception for Jewish soldiers. That spring the Knights of Columbus opened a downtown center to entertain Roman Catholic sailors and soldiers. Jacksonville women took part in a host of activities. Many joined the local Red Cross chapter, which engaged in first aid, nursing, hospitality, and relief activities. They distributed food, clothing, and other supplies to area families adversely affected by the war. In addition, volunteers made, packaged, and shipped abroad more than 500,000 surgical dressings, plus bathrobes, pajamas, bed shirts, surgeon's gowns, hot-water-bottle covers, operating sheets, pillowcases, napkins, facecloths, towels, and handkerchiefs. Under pressure from Washington, local Red Cross officials asked the Reverend John E. Ford of Bethel Baptist Institutional Church to form a colored chapter. Meanwhile Eartha White organized black club women for the war effort. In addition to establishing a Liberty Kitchen at Stanton High School to teach about food substitutes and conserving fuels, she organized young black women for employment as elevator operators, bellhops, and chauffeurs, in jobs that opened to blacks because of labor shortages. Further, she organized a Mutual Protection League for Working Girls to ensure that the new workers were not taken advantage of. Alice Dunbar Nelson, field representative for the Woman's Committee of the Council of National Defense, praised White's work as director of the best black state woman's committee in the South.[14]

With the construction of Camp Johnston and the arrival of the first of 27,000 military personnel, orders for goods and services had a growing impact on the Jacksonville economy. Fully recovered from the 1914–16 depression, the economy began to boom. Shipbuilding was a major stimulus. Of eight yards, Merrill-Stevens Company was the largest, doubling its size with the construction of new facilities on the south bank of the St. Johns River (near where Assumption Catholic Church and Bishop Kenney High School now stand). The number of employees jumped from 642 in 1916 to 3,839 by August 1918, making it the largest firm in the city. About half the employees were blacks; all worked nine-hour days, six days per week. An estimated 10,000 men and women were employed in all of the city's shipyards. Shipbuilding, in turn, stimulated work in machine shops, foundries, and iron works. Shortages of skilled workers nationally prompted raids from the Charleston, South Carolina, shipyards, while higher wages helped inflate prices locally. The cost of living rose 63 percent between 1914 and September 1917, and another 21 percent from December 1917 to October 1918, despite efforts by the Federal Food Administration to check prices. With jobs plentiful, newcomers, mostly whites, moved to Jacksonville. Where two years earlier the city had a surfeit of housing, by November 1917 there was a shortage. The local Real Estate Exchange attempted to block rent gouging, but with only limited success. Inflation became painful, particularly for local residents on fixed incomes. The city council tried to ease the discomfort by raising salaries for city employees, and the school board, at the recommendation of Superintendent Hathaway, increased teachers' salaries.[15]

To meet the housing shortage for shipyard workers, the Chamber of Commerce in August 1918 proposed and the United States Shipping Board Emergency Fleet Corporation initiated the construction of a public housing project in South Jacksonville near the Merrill Stevens facility. It was designed by architect Henry Klutho and named after Florida's senior United States senator. Fletcher Park comprised 158 two-, three-, and four-bedroom "bungalow-type" stucco houses on Atlantic Boulevard and adjacent streets just west of the Florida East Coast Railroad. The war ended, however, before construction was completed.[16]

Meanwhile Jacksonville's young men and women marched off to war, though sometimes reluctantly. In an August 1917 draft call of 553 men, one-quarter (142) were rejected as physically unfit. Another two-fifths (239) claimed exemptions based on marriage or family, leaving 172 men (or less than one-third of the total) to serve. That same month military recruiters arrived in Jacksonville seeking African-American volunteers as navy mess attendants and army hospital corpsmen. In September 550 national guardsmen departed for active duty, leaving the Home Guard to maintain order locally. In all, 4,942 Duval County residents (three-quarters draftees) served their country. Of that number, 157 (108 whites and 49 blacks) paid the ultimate price.[17]

In April 1918 a contingent of 2,500 black troops arrived at Camp Johnston, housed in quarters segregated from the white quartermaster trainees. They were almost all Florida draftees, originally scheduled to train at Fort Devons, Massachusetts. A black YMCA was organized to provide recreational programs, and Jacksonville's black community volunteered to help. Still, incidents arose. Following the armistice in November, the morale officer reported an attempt by fifty black soldiers to break out of a detention camp. Sentries shot two, killing one of them. Camp officials responded by trying to improve recreational and athletic facilities for the soldiers where training had essentially ceased and time lay heavily on largely idle hands. In December the enlisted men of Remount Squadron #349 appealed to the camp's commanding general about inadequate food, a disrespectful junior officer, and a company commander who did not explain his orders. The junior officer, they wrote, "talk[ed] to us like a dog," promised them only beans to eat, and threatened to court-martial anyone who complained to the commanding officer. Again, the base morale officer investigated, this time reporting that the complaints centered on three or four men, not the entire squadron. The surviving records at the National Archives do not speak further to the conditions of the African-American soldiers at Camp Johnston, but with the war over, training largely for disciplinary purposes, white officers, and a camp bordering on a deep South city, conditions probably were less than ideal.[18]

□ While the first year of the war saw Jacksonvillians enthusiastically volunteering to conserve food and energy, entertaining trainees at Camp Johnston, and subscribing to liberty bonds, the second year saw a change of mood. The positive voluntary support continued, but along with it developed a coercive atmosphere to force conformity and suppress dissent. Both voluntary and coercive efforts took place following the formation of a Liberty League on the anniversary of war's declaration. Sponsors included Mayor Martin, city councilman John T. Alsop, Francis Conroy and Telfair Stockton from the Chamber of Commerce, and Nina Cummer and Lina Barnett from the Woman's Club. The league also provided for a secret vigilance committee of ten men and ten women instructed to look for "all pro-German or disloyal utterances and acts, and to provide for the suppression of the same in the most effective manner in harmony with Americanism."[19]

Two days earlier, on April 4, 1918, an unidentified group had chiseled

Jacksonville Freight Yards. Courtesy of the Haydon Burns Library.

the name "Germania" from the cornerstone of the old Germania Club building, now the Metropolitan Club. On April 8 the league's vigilance committee told the city's German Lutheran churches to conduct all services in English. Wherever there were signs in German, they should be removed. A week later other vigilantes charged a German-born dairyman with making pro-German utterances, stripped off his shirt, smeared him with tar and feathers, and made him salute an American flag. That summer the city council passed legislation (later declared unconstitutional) prohibiting German aliens from handling food or drink in the city.[20]

Liberty League women next began recruiting children in the schools as well as women in department stores and other businesses. For the young people organized into a Junior Patriotic League, they drafted a set of bylaws. Article One set standards of behavior:

> 1. obedience to parents, teachers, local and national government;
>
> 2. economy in food (not to waste any), clothes (not abuse them, but dress simply), amusements (select them carefully and be moderate in attendance), property (do not abuse or destroy your own or other people's), and money (buy War Savings stamps);
>
> 3. respect for one's self (guard your conduct), the rights of others (be polite and considerate), time (do not waste it), health (take care of it), flag (reverence it), and government (do not criticize it);
>
> 4. prudence in conduct (avoid vulgarity in speech and act), and conversation (talk victory and report sedition);

5. work in the Junior Patriotic League, Junior Red Cross, Boy Scouts and War Savings societies; and

6. loyalty to Jacksonville (love and protect your city), Florida (make it the best state in the union), our country, the U.S. of A. (defend it, talk for it, work for it, help win the war).[21]

Liberty Leaguer Corita Doggett, daughter of a local judge who was also commander of the Home Guards, proposed that each evening at 6 o'clock, buglers in different parts of the city should sound "to the colors." Everyone would stop whatever he or she was doing. Men would remove their hats, and in homes, offices, and shops across the city, people would stand silently and renew their patriotic pledge. A *Times-Union* editorial compared it to Catholics observing the Angelus or the Muslim call to prayer. In effect, Miss Doggett's proposal virtually made patriotism a religion for Americans. People would worship their nation without question, with devotion, commitment, and self-sacrifice.[22]

Doggett's proposal was praised but not implemented. Instead, city councilman (and later six-term mayor) John T. Alsop introduced, and the council passed, an ordinance requiring all Jacksonvillians to honor the American flag daily. According to the ordinance, at 6:00 P.M. each day "Big Jim," the waterworks whistle, which could be heard across most of the city, would blow one long and one short blast. All persons would stop what they were doing for one minute. Traffic would stop; all men would remove their hats; and flags would be lowered to complete the observance. The penalty for noncompliance was a reprimand by the local judge, presumably Miss Doggett's father, and possibly an unofficial visit from vigilantes.[23]

That summer the Liberty League's secret vigilance committee reported local shopkeepers who were selling penny candy with prizes inside. Many of the prizes were pasteboard representations of the German Iron Cross and the Austrian Order of the Golden Fleece. Upon investigation, the committee discovered that a Newark, New Jersey, firm had unloaded these goods on naive local dealers. The shopkeepers were told to destroy their stock of candy and pasteboard prizes.[24]

Not all of the Liberty League's efforts went toward promoting religious patriotism or ferreting out potential subversion. The league provided workers for liberty bond drives and 200 volunteers for Red Cross service. They made 300 patriotic speeches; organized eleven neighborhood chapters and Liberty Leagues outside Jacksonville; visited every school, recruiting thousands of school children; and assisted the food and fuel administrator to encourage conservation of scarce resources. They also helped find jobs for women to replace men gone off to war, searched for obscene literature, and encouraged black community groups to organize to save food and fuel. The Liberty League itself, however, had only white members.[25]

That summer streetcar workers struck seeking union recognition and increased pay. The traction company responded by offering raises but refusing to recognize the union. Fifteen Liberty League women volunteered to become streetcar conductors to keep the trolleys running. When the strikers hooted and called them scabs, the women became upset and told their husbands and fathers, who put pressure on the mayor to provide police protection for the transit company. The mayor, previously considered pro-labor, ordered the police into action, and the streetcars ran. The workers eventually received their wage increases, but not union recognition. The Liberty League intervention helped to break the strike.[26]

That fall the Liberty League announced plans to enforce prohibition by tearing down all liquor signs. Members also offered to identify idlers unwilling to work for the war effort and enforce the flag ordinance to ensure that motorists stopped when Big Jim's whistle blew. They urged the residents of the New Berlin community in Duval County to change its name. In September the city council introduced a "work or fight" bill, aimed at blacks, requiring every able-bodied male between the ages of fifteen and fifty-five to work as part of the war effort. Slackers would be fined $30 or thirty days. In October hooded vigilantes, reminiscent of the Ku Klux Klan, marched through downtown intimidating residents to buy war bonds in the fourth Liberty Loan campaign. The coercive character of the Liberty League eased with the signing of the Armistice on November 11, but not entirely. By mid-1919 it had found a new villain in the Russian Revolution, and pledged itself to "suppress Bolshevism in America."[27]

The efforts of Jacksonville's Liberty League to both promote support for the war effort and suppress possible opposition were characteristic of citizen groups across the country. Fortunately, Jacksonville escaped the excesses that resulted in the lynching of a German-American near St. Louis or an I.W.W. official in Butte, Montana. Still, dissent was discouraged, as the local dairy farmer discovered. Efforts to shape a common or single vision of American patriotism, especially among schoolchildren, seemed to meet the needs of the war effort and had popular support. Yet, over the longer term, it denied to nonconformists, whether striking workers, immigrants, minorities, or pacifists, their freedom to dissent under the Constitution's Bill of Rights. Equally important, such a single

Camp Joseph E. Johnston. Courtesy of the Haydon Burns Library.

national vision, if coerced, had the capacity to stifle the growth and development of an entire civilization.[28]

□ The second year of the war also saw the arrival of the Spanish influenza epidemic to the United States. It came to Jacksonville in September 1918, infecting inmates at the city prison farm. On October 1, according to city health officer Dr. William W. MacDonnell, it became an epidemic. MacDonnell issued warnings in the city's newspapers. He urged residents to avoid crowds, identified symptoms, and recommended medicinal dosages for relief. On October 7 Superintendent Hathaway, after conferring with MacDonnell, closed the city and county schools. The next day the city council passed legislation empowering the city commission to close all places of amusement, which it did. Theaters, cinemas, pool halls, dance halls, soda fountains, and cigar stores closed their doors. Shop hours were restricted and all public assemblies were banned. Funeral services were limited to immediate family and clergy. That weekend no church or synagogue held services. Downtown looked deserted. Signs hanging on many shop doors simply stated "all sick."[29]

On October 10 the first soup kitchen opened at the Union Congregational Church to provide emergency food. Another opened at Stanton High School under the direction of Eartha White. Club women formed a Health Relief Association to deliver meals to shut-ins and serve the walk-ins. At Camp Johnston Major General William P. Duvall loaned four portable army soup kitchens to feed hungry people. For twelve days healthy volunteers fed 5,709 white and 11,084 black victims of the influenza. Meanwhile emergency hospitals were opened at the YMCA, YMHA, Stanton School, and St. Luke's Hospital.[30]

The epidemic lasted about a month. By the end of October, Camp Johnston soldiers were back in town. Churches and synagogues had reopened. Children returned to school on November 4. By Armistice Day the city's mood could shift from anxiety to celebration, except for families grieving deceased members. City health officer MacDonnell estimated that one-third of the population, or about 30,000 people, had contracted the flu, causing 464 deaths. Local historian T. Frederick Davis compared it to the 427 deaths during the yellow fever epidemic of 1888, which stretched over four months instead of one, but in a much smaller city. This time there was no panic. Instead, "the rattle of the death carts of 1888 was supplanted by the whir of the motor in 1918, as the trucks took their loads away."[31]

Comparisons of Jacksonville's epidemic with other cities are difficult. Philadelphia and San Francisco had particularly virulent attacks of the flu that year. Tampa's scourge came later in November and was less severe.[32]

□ The signing of the Armistice ended World War I on November 11, 1918. Local historian T. Frederick Davis described the Jacksonville scene:

> From the first blast of "Big Jim" (the waterworks whistle) at 3 AM of the 11th, announcing the signing of the armistice, until early morning of the 12th, Jacksonville reveled in continuous celebration. Parades without number formed and marched, merged with other processions and disbanded from exhaustion, only to rest and form again. Every noise-making instrument in the city worked overtime. Whistles of the mills, the river craft, Big Jim, and the South Jacksonville siren rent the air at irregular intervals; automobiles tore through the city streets each dragging from one to six garbage cans, dish pans, tin buckets,—anything to heighten the clatter. The 11th was declared a holiday by the city, county, and every business firm in the locality. Throughout the day enthusiastic crowds thronged the streets. Soldiers from Camp Johnston were everywhere, as a holiday had also been declared by the commander of the camp. A great organized parade was held on the 12th. Companies from Camp Johnston, the Duval County home guards, civic organizations, shipyard workers, any body of people that could be assembled, joined in. There may have been larger demonstrations in the centers of

greater population than Jacksonville, but for all-round enthusiasm the celebration here could not have been exceeded and the residents of Jacksonville at the time will never forget it.[33]

Demobilization at Camp Johnston began almost immediately. By early 1919 only a rear guard remained to close up and maintain records. Senator Fletcher wrote to the general manager of the Emergency Fleet Corporation urging a gradual cancellation of shipbuilding contracts to avoid simply throwing men and women out of work. Construction of Fletcher Park homes continued until completion, but they were never fully occupied at this time. Their location next to the Merrill Stevens yards, which were cutting back employment, offered little incentive. In addition, in the absence of public transportation, they were a twenty-minute, one-and-a-quarter-mile walk to the ferry that crossed the St. Johns River to downtown Jacksonville. City workers could find housing closer to their places of employment.[34]

Postwar cutbacks by the federal government apparently did not hurt Jacksonville's economy. Instead, local construction postponed for the duration picked up the slack. The Duval County Commission prepared for the bond sale and building of the St. Johns River (later Acosta) Bridge authorized before the war. Construction of the new Union Depot railroad station (subsequently restored as the Prime Osborne Convention Center in the 1980s) got underway. City programs for street paving, parks, and sewers, also postponed, were now funded. Private developers resumed building homes in the suburbs. The Cummer phosphate plant, whose exports to the continent had been banned as contraband during the war, loaded its first ship bound for Europe in five years. Joseph Golden and Company and other film producers spoke of making motion pictures in Jacksonville once again. Armour and Company announced a million-dollar addition to its packing plant, and two new movie theaters opened their doors. To oversee a renewed public/private expansion of Jacksonville's economy, the Chamber of Commerce resumed monthly meetings in 1919 after a wartime hiatus, and joined with the Real Estate Board, Rotary, and Automobile Club to undertake a national public relations campaign on behalf of the city's growth and development.[35]

Many Jacksonville residents, like their counterparts across the country, looked forward to a return to what President Warren G. Harding would soon call "normalcy." Work and play, family and friends, and a renewed prosperity would resume as in "the good old days." The arrival of the

Col. Fred L. Munson, commanding officer, and his staff at Camp Joseph E. Johnston. Courtesy of the Haydon Burns Library.

Brooklyn Dodgers and New York Yankees for spring training seemed to fulfill this anticipation.[36]

Local citizens and voluntary associations also looked to continue improving Jacksonville's quality of life. Liberty League members, with affiliate chapters across the city, sought to resume the work of the old neighborhood civic associations beautifying schoolyards, supporting street paving, caring for the needy, and encouraging involvement in community issues. The Jacksonville Rotary asked the city council to buy land in Riverside on the St. Johns River for a memorial park, which it did. The Real Estate Board in cooperation with Rotary and the chamber pushed for a municipal golf course. Kiwanis organized its first chapter in Duval County, as did the Jacksonville Business and Professional Woman's Club, as part of the national federation. Meanwhile Associated Charities, the Tuberculosis Association, Children's Home Society, Boys Home, and YM and YWCAs formed the Duval County Council of Social Agencies.[37]

In the public sector, the Duval County School Board again raised teachers' salaries, and Superintendent Hathaway proposed building two junior high schools to accommodate the overflow of students at the city's one white high school. Mayor Martin, reelected in May, introduced a bill to extend city boundaries in residential areas to the north and west in anticipation of the 1920 census. Meanwhile former state senator Telfair Stockton, having introduced a bill in 1917 to consolidate city and county governments, urged the Jacksonville Real Estate Board to support fresh efforts to streamline local government for greater efficiency. A city-county committee began work to secure a landing field for an army air corps air mail route, and a *Times-Union* editorial advocated Jacksonville becoming the gateway for trade with Latin America.[38]

On the surface, the reversion of this New South city to economic and civic development appeared to go smoothly. But other issues troubled Jacksonville residents. Inflation was one of them. Another was a series of strikes that disrupted labor-management relations and the New South image. Shipyard workers struck the Merrill Stevens Company in March and again in October. Communications workers picketed the telephone company in April and then at Western Union. In June the city firefighters struck followed by the railroad workers and cigar makers in August. The two most disruptive strikes were at Western Union and by the firefighters.[39]

The Western Union strike, part of a nationwide protest, began when local company officials allegedly infiltrated the union with spies, leading to the dismissal of sixty-five employees. Following strikers' threats to nonstriking workers, the company obtained a court order restraining them. Despite the injunction, a mob of about 100 strikers and sympathizers beat up a nonstriker in front of the Western Union office and threw rocks through company windows. Mayor Martin sympathized with the strikers and claimed the local media exaggerated the incident. Three weeks later Martin dismissed three police officers for taking money from Western Union officials and attacked the firm for offering bribes. The workers were eventually reinstated.[40]

The firefighters' strike split city government and the community. The men had joined the International Association of Fire Fighters, an affiliate of the American Federation of Labor. The city commission acquiesced in this action, provided job discipline remained unaffected. The new union's grievance committee replied that they risked life and limb for the city, and they would act as they saw fit. The commission responded by suspending the members of the grievance committee and firing the head of the union, without hearing or cause. The next day the city's firefighters struck en masse. The *Times-Union* editors called it a strike against the people, bordering on treason, and the fire chief began hiring replacements. Prominent citizens volunteered their services while the strikers promised to come back and fight if any serious fires broke out.[41]

Meanwhile, city council members began investigating the conflict and concluded that the men were right. They organized because they felt their chief did not represent them adequately to the city commission, and they could not communicate in any other way. The commission responded by claiming the council lacked jurisdiction in the dispute. The council then began a recall of commission members, securing some 5,127 signatures for an election. Next, Governor Sidney Catts came over from Tallahassee and joined with Mayor Martin in support of the strikers and for recall of the commission. Eventually the commissioners conceded, reinstated the men, and the strike came to an end.[42]

The local labor-management strife occurring in the context of state, regional, and national strikes seemed to many Jacksonville (and other American) citizens to reflect a rising tide of Bolshevism. Across the country, 1919 was the year of the Red Scare. The general strike in Seattle, the police strike in Boston, the steel strike nationwide, and other disruptions persuaded many middle-class Americans that radicals had taken over the labor movement, threatening the very foundations of the free enterprise system. Local, state, and federal officials responded by carrying forward their wartime patriotism into a postwar suppression of radicals, workers, foreigners, minorities, and immigrants—anyone who seemed to challenge the existing order. In Jacksonville concerned citizens organized a Central Liberty League to "suppress Bolshevism." It was to this group that former United States Senator Nathan P. Bryan spoke of "no place for the red flag of anarchy in the United States." That fall Attorney General A. Mitchell Palmer began his campaign against alleged subversives across the nation. On January 2, 1920, when his agents arrested hundreds of men and women across the country, eight Jacksonville residents were caught. It was the only city in the Southeast in which raids took place.[43]

In the home of J. A. Adams, a machinist at the Merrill Stevens shipyard, agents found a district charter for the Communist Labor Party, a minute book of the local party chapter, speeches by socialist leader Eugene V. Debs, "as well as several books printed in Yiddish and Russian." Abe Weisselman, a thirty-year-old plumber, also was arrested, en route home from the Jacksonville labor temple. He had a membership card in the Communist Labor Party. Such were the exaggerated fears of middle-class Americans who saw the need to arrest eight local workers as conspirators to overthrow the entire economic and political system.[44]

Workers were not the only Americans with grievances in 1919. African-

YWCA Hostess House at Camp Joseph E. Johnston. Courtesy of the Haydon Burns Library.

Americans coming home from fighting a war to make a world safe for democracy had theirs as well. In Jacksonville black teachers petitioned the school board on a series of issues. They wanted equal pay with white teachers. The recent raises to both blacks and whites had increased already existing discrepancies. Second, they wanted summer institutes similar to those provided white teachers in order to improve their teaching skills. Third, they wanted a black supervisor to work with and assist black teachers, as in white schools. None existed at the time. Fourth, they wanted appointments in the spring term for the following year, just as for whites, so they could make plans and know whether they would be employed. Ninety percent of black teachers taught in classrooms with more than fifty pupils and they felt the school motto for them was "more work, less pay."[45]

Beginning in May and extending across the summer, black and white America exploded in violence. July was particularly tense with race riots in Omaha, Chicago, and Washington, D.C. In the Windy City, thirty-eight people were killed and more than five hundred injured. In the heat of August, two Jacksonville African-Americans, Bowman Cook and John Morine, allegedly murdered George Du Bose, a young white, well-known insurance supervisor whose company sold policies to Jacksonville blacks. What DuBose was doing in the black community that night, the newspapers did not say. The *Times-Union* did report, however, the attack as the second within a month of blacks upon whites in Jacksonville. A few days later *Times-Union* readers learned of racial violence in Knoxville following the alleged murder of a white woman by a black man. Meanwhile, in Jacksonville, whites took the law into their own hands. On September 7 a band of twenty-five to thirty men overpowered the jailer, took Cook and Morine from their cells, and carried them north of the city. Both were killed. Morine's body was riddled with bullets and dumped in a ditch. Cook's body was tied to the rear bumper of an automobile, dragged into town, and dumped in front of the fashionable Windsor Hotel across from Hemming Park.[46]

Authorities feared an escalation of violence as in other cities, but none occurred. The next day the *Times-Union* reported, "the city is serene after lynching of two negroes." Reporters learned that the mob was not a raucous one, but rather a band of men determined to avenge the death of their friend. The police, however, arrested no one. The media condemned the lynching as did the Ministerial Alliance, Chamber of Commerce, Real Estate Board, Rotary, Kiwanis, and Bar Association, in part because it threatened race relations and caused a bad image nationally for the city.[47]

Jacksonville's black clergy responded with a full-page advertisement in the newspaper protesting the action in the most diplomatic terms. "The hitherto good feeling between the two races in Jacksonville has been somewhat strained," they said. "Incidents have happened which all good citizens regret, incidents calculated to make us forget that wise thinking, and the best judgement are always necessary at such a time as this." From New York, James Weldon Johnson was less restrained. The two lynchings for him measured the deterioration of race relations in his native state since his youth. "One . . . is taken up entirely with the shame of the city," he wrote in *The New York Age*. Johnson approved the Chamber of Commerce's declaration that Jacksonville was not a "lynch law community," but later observed that a number of leading blacks of the city had been notified that they must leave. Clearly, Jacksonville was reasserting with vigor the white supremacy doctrine of this New South city.[48]

The final area of disturbance expressed itself in a concern for the rapid growth in South Florida. In May a *Times-Union* editorial quoted northern real estate people about how Jacksonville lacked apartments comparable to Miami's, which attracted tourists for longer visits. Another editorial quoted a Pennsylvania newspaper attributing Miami's new prominence to its being the best advertised city in the state. Again, a visitor back from "the magic city" expressed amazement with its rapid growth. There is a feeling, he said, that Jacksonville capitalists are too timid compared to their Miami, St. Petersburg, and West Palm Beach counterparts.[49]

The Chamber of Commerce tried to counter this growing image. Its

YMCA Building at Camp Joseph E. Johnston. Courtesy of the Haydon Burns Library.

new Committee of Fifteen developed an advertising campaign to spend $100,000 per year for five years to sell Jacksonville nationally. The *Times-Union* endorsed the plan, but complained that local business people did not work together and act as forthrightly as Miamians. This concern for Jacksonville factionalism surfaced several times. One Miami hotel man commented, "Undercurrents in Jacksonville . . . keep the businessmen apart and there was very little pulling together . . . for the general good." The *Times-Union* agreed.[50]

Meanwhile the effort to expand the city's boundaries reflected competition with Tampa and a concern to maintain Jacksonville's status as Florida's first city. There were concerns about momentum despite the year of general prosperity. The strikes seemed to hurt. There was also this factionalism, alluded to but not explained. Was it between old guard and new, or between local and national corporate interests? Finally, there was the energy and ambition of South Florida developers combined with the year-round attractions that Flagler had initiated pushing his railroad south from St. Augustine to Palm Beach, Miami, and Key West. All of these concerns hovered just over the horizon as Jacksonville converted to peace in the year after the Armistice.

□ American involvement in World War I lasted only nineteen months, but it shook Jacksonville just as it jarred the nation. Mobilization directed from Washington boosted the city's economy in its twentieth-century drive toward material prosperity. At the same time, the war hysteria hardened the city's idealistic spirit in its pursuit of a 100 percent patriotism, intolerant of diversity. The war brought forth much idealism and generous effort on the part of volunteers helping servicemen and women, refugees, and flu victims; yet it also produced a rigidity in values that fostered prohibition. Tentative efforts by whites to cooperate with blacks on behalf of the war effort resulted in small steps forward on liberty bond drives, food and fuel conservation, and hospitality for soldiers, provided blacks kept their place. The end result was to further foster New South economic prosperity and maintain white supremacy. It also made more callous the spirit of idealism that once tolerated and cared for others who dared to be different.

SEVEN

Jacksonville as a New South City

By the end of World War I, Jacksonville had become a New South city. The vision of Henry Grady as expanded by subsequent journalists, educators, businessmen, and politicians fit the Gateway City. While its population more than tripled from 28,249 in 1900 to 91,558 in 1920, property values increased almost eight times. The number of workers engaged in manufacturing rose four times; the value of their products, thirteen times. Bank deposits multiplied fifteen times, and bank clearings, reflecting local and regional commerce, increased almost fiftyfold. Exports were sixty-one times greater than a generation earlier; imports, 188 times. Ships, once limited to coastal trade because of a shallow riverbed, now sailed up a thirty-foot channel and across the ocean to Europe, or south through the Caribbean to Cuba and Latin America.[1]

Travelers to Jacksonville most often arrived at the handsome new neoclassical depot on one of the more than 100 passenger trains daily. Once detrained, they could hire a taxi or ride the trolley downtown to modern hotels, department stores, high-rise office buildings, or theaters. Businessmen might return home to the attractive suburbs of Riverside or Springfield. The image of the city on the St. Johns River with its new automotive bridge under construction reflected a busy, prosperous, growing, modern metropolis.

As part of the economic development, Jacksonvillians did not neglect the public sector. They invested substantially in their public schools to prepare youngsters for the next generation. They took part in the national movement to improve public health conditions, which resulted in a substantial reduction in the local mortality rates for both infants and adults. They followed urban reformers in other cities setting aside park land and developing recreational programs. They also introduced civil service reform to the police and fire departments as well as a modified city commission to foster more efficient democratic city government. They supported child labor reform, woman's suffrage, and prohibition. The scope of development was broad. It fit into the context of the Progressive Movement underway nationally during these years, led by Theodore Roosevelt and Woodrow Wilson. The changes also affected the public-private partnerships of local government with business and professional men, club women, neighborhood civic associations, and religious groups in Jacksonville as well as in other cities across the nation. The results were reflected in the development of public policy at the local, state, and national levels during the era.[2]

Jacksonville's women played a substantial role in this development through their clubs and churches. They studied urban problems, proposed reforms, and lobbied for appropriate legislation. Children were their particular concern in areas of health care, education, work rules, parks, and recreation. Yet they also developed programs to help poor people, tuberculars, and the elderly. They even reached tentatively across racial lines in efforts to serve the entire community. Their lack of both political and economic power made their achievements more remarkable. In effect, Jacksonville's women had to persuade the male establishment at the board/chamber, City Hall, and state house to accept a broader definition of economic development for the New South, to include what later generations would call quality-of-life issues. In this achievement these women, while not yet achieving equality for themselves, became part of the New South city.

Meanwhile economic development also influenced the changing character of Jacksonville's popular culture. Entrepreneurs built amusement parks, beach resorts, movie theaters, and department stores for commerce and entertainment. Newspaper editors and publishers broadened reader horizons, encouraging the purchase of automobiles, fashionable clothing, suburban homes, and other consumables. As the city grew, popular tastes changed. People were encouraged to spend more, play more, and seek

City as viewed from Hemming Park. Reprinted from Caroline Rawls, comp., *The Jacksonville Story*, 35.

status through what they acquired. Traditional values were challenged and conflicts resulted. During these years Jacksonville, like other New South cities, became increasingly part of twentieth-century urban America.[3]

The African-American community, though segregated, also participated in the city's broad-based economic development. By 1920 blacks owned a bank, an insurance company, a weekly newspaper, two movie theaters, and a host of small businesses. Blacks operated half the city's barber shops, over half the dry cleaners, 86 restaurants, and 114 retail groceries. They were lawyers, doctors, dentists, and teachers as well as broom manufacturers, cigar makers, bicycle and automobile repairmen, jewelers, undertakers, printers, tailors, and dressmakers.[4]

Frequently excluded from the public sector, African-Americans developed their voluntary associations to serve their community. Their number of churches almost doubled during these years. So did the number of their fraternal lodges. Blacks built a handsome masonic temple on Broad Street, which is still standing in the 1990s, plus halls for the Knights of Pythias, Odd Fellows, and carpenters' union. Black women organized their associations. Blacks also organized a local chapter of the National Negro Business League and the National Association for the Advancement of Colored People. They belonged to statewide colored teachers,

Wellington W. Cummer, Jacksonville's leading businessman and largest employer. Reprinted from Daniel Pleasant Gold, *History of Duval County, Florida*, 458.

medical, and bar associations. After the fire, they rebuilt Edward Waters College, Florida Baptist Academy, and Cookman Institute. They also ran their own hospital.[6]

Where possible, blacks took part in the public sector. They lobbied for parks and new schools for their community, and persuaded the school board to build the new brick Stanton Graded and High School. They cooperated with the health department to improve community conditions. Particularly noteworthy was the reduction in infant mortality. Black club women served their community and also cooperated with white club women on a variety of social projects. During the war young blacks served in the military, and members of the community bought liberty bonds. Jacksonville's black community took part in the New South development of Jacksonville to the extent their resources and the white community permitted.

Henry Grady's second major emphasis for the New South, besides economic development, was regional reconciliation in which southerners welcomed northern businessmen and entrepreneurs to invest in the region. This, too, happened in Jacksonville. Charles Garner came from Indiana to become first a riverboat captain, later eight-time president of

Joseph E. Blodgett, Jacksonville's most prominent African-American businessman. Courtesy of the Carpenter Library, University of North Florida.

the Board of Trade and bank president. William Barnett arrived from Kansas to establish what became Jacksonville's largest bank. Francis Conroy moved from Chicago as a sales representative for Armour and Company, later organized his own meat-packing firm, headed the Board of Trade, and provided leadership in a variety of other civic activities. Henry Klutho, the city's premier architect, came from New York. Dr. Charles Terry, the progressive health officer, was born in Connecticut and earned his medical degree at the University of Maryland in Baltimore before coming to Jacksonville. John A. Gregg, president of Edward Waters College and later bishop in the AME Church, was born and educated in Kansas. Annie Broward, wife of the governor, and later active as a businesswoman, club president, school board member, and member of the recreation board, came from New York City. Perhaps the Cummer family from Michigan epitomized the contributions of the northern newcomers. The father became the city's largest employer with his sawmill and later phosphate plant north of town. He also took an active role in the Board of Trade, lobbied in Washington for a deeper river channel, supported numerous charitable efforts, and helped found the YMCA. His wife, meanwhile, worked through the Woman's Club for better public schools and parks. Both sons and their wives carried on their parents' active role to improve conditions in Jacksonville.

To recognize these northern contributions does not mean ignoring

Annie Douglass Broward, governor's wife, businesswoman, and civic activist. Reprinted from Daniel Pleasant Gold, *History of Duval County, Florida*, 283.

local leaders, or the role of newcomers to Jacksonville from the South. Two-time mayor J. E. T. Bowden spent his early years in South Carolina, as did the Reverend Elias Gregg, pastor of Mt. Zion AME Church. Mayor and later United States Senator Duncan Fletcher, black contractor Joseph Blodgett, and state senator Ion Farris came from Georgia. The Stockton brothers, May Mann Jennings, Philip Randolph, and school superintendent Fons Hathaway were born or grew up in small-town or rural Florida. Jacob Cohen, the department store magnate, came from Dublin, Ireland, and James Weldon Johnson's mother was born in Nassau. The list could go on. Clearly, the city utilized the talents of people from many places for its economic and urban development.[6]

Grady's third concern for the New South city was for racial reconciliation in which African-Americans would vote, have the protection of the law, and progress under the paternalistic tutelage of benevolent white southerners. There were some benevolent white southerners. James Weldon Johnson in his autobiography referred to Dr. John C. L'Engle, physician, banker, and state senator, and Duncan Fletcher as fair whites. Among the club women, May Jennings worked closely with Eartha White on social issues beneficial to both blacks and whites. But, sadly, these people were the exceptions, as L'Engle himself told Johnson. The latter remembered the following conversation upon his return from his consulship in Nicaragua in 1913.[7] "He [L'Engle] talked to me for some minutes about my father, in the characteristically terse manner for which he was well known in Jacksonville. He told me, too, that he had attended my father's funeral. . . . Then quite abruptly he asked, 'Do you intend to stay in Jacksonville?' I replied that I was not sure. He then said, 'You can't do it. If you had never gone away, it would be a different matter. But Jacksonville is not the Jacksonville you used to know. Don't try it.' "

□ While many Jacksonville blacks aspired to the values of the New South with hard work and clean living, white-black relations deteriorated in the generation after the fire, as they did across the region. The state legislature passed the white primary law in 1901. Also in that year, the city council segregated Jacksonville's streetcars. Black community leaders protested, but to no avail. They then boycotted the streetcars and challenged the ordinance in court. An initial court victory was subsequently nullified by passage of a statewide law. In 1907 local government excluded African-Americans from all but the most menial city jobs. Also that year the legislature gerrymandered the council election districts in Jacksonville, eliminating black representation. African-Americans would not again sit on the city council until the 1960s.

The city's political leaders were not the only suppressors of blacks. When local blacks celebrated the victory of heavyweight champion Jack Johnson in 1910, whites rioted, attacking the celebrants and destroying black-owned properties. In 1914 the president of the Colored Board of Trade appealed to the president of the Jacksonville Board of Trade for help in controlling the city police. "Thirty or more colored men had been shot down by police officers recently," he wrote. When younger blacks began migrating North just before the war, city officials first tried to persuade, then coerce them into staying. During the war troubles continued, climaxed by the lynchings of 1919. Clearly conditions had worsened. Ambitious blacks, such as Johnson, Philip Randolph, and Milton Waldron, left Jacksonville to become part of the New Negro movement in the Harlem Renaissance and other northern cities. White hostility and suppression became a heavy cross to bear for Jacksonville blacks remaining in the city. Grady's optimism about race relations and the benevolence of white southerners was mistaken.[8]

What happened to white-black relations in Jacksonville took place across the South during these years. Historian Joel Williamson in his com-

Telfair Stockton, prominent suburban developer. Courtesy of Wayne W. Wood.

prehensive study of the era describes a shift in the "mentality," or mindset of white southerners. They always believed in white supremacy. But in earlier years they, like Grady, believed in helping blacks like Johnson or Booker T. Washington to better themselves and their people. Beginning around 1890, however, these attitudes changed. Increasingly, many white southerners saw blacks as almost subhuman people who must be suppressed, if not removed from society. Part of the reason for the shift came out of the economic dislocations of the era. As the southern farm population grew, cotton prices fell and the land could not support the people. Attempts to seek relief through the Farmers Alliances or Populist Party failed. With depression and greater poverty came increased crime. Repeatedly, the white-owned press depicted black crimes of violence, including rape. Although the reports were greatly exaggerated, whites panicked. In the Victorian morality of the New South, rape was an attack upon the purity of womanhood, particularly the sanctity of white women. In the stress of hard times, whites unable to resolve their economic problems projected their frustrations and anger toward blacks. They became the scapegoats for all of white society's ills, and therefore the target of white hatred and violence, including castrations and lynchings.[9]

In Jacksonville the shift in white attitudes toward blacks is not well documented except in James Weldon Johnson's autobiography. Clearly state policy enacting the poll tax, the white primary, segregated streetcars, and gerrymandered council districts reflected the feelings and dominance of North Florida's white rural legislators in the state capital. It also reflected local attitudes that hardened over the decades. Jacksonville was not without its stress. Industrial development, expansion of the port and railroads with their shipyards and maintenance shops, and the growth of residential and commercial construction brought opportunities but also dislocations. Available jobs attracted an influx of blacks and whites from across Florida, Georgia, and other southern states, who brought with them their racial views. Historian I. A. Newby has described the values of these southern white "plain folk," many of whom came to Jacksonville. "This was a time of racial extremism and pervasive racial consciousness among nearly all white southerners. . . . Like other groups in the New South, folk learned racism and racial awareness at an early age and acted out their beliefs as circumstances dictated."[10]

What once had been a small tourist, banking, and transport city dominated by a small, mostly native white elite supportive of relatively open racial relations became a medium-sized commercial and industrial metropolis bent on excluding blacks from substantial roles. The stress of the depression beginning in 1914 doubtless had its impact. The black outmigration began the following year. The war brought more white migrants and a white majority to the city. The lynchings in 1919 reflected the culmination of race hatred locally in a year in which racial violence and the Red Scare made national headlines.[11]

Yet despite the hardening of white attitudes, Jacksonville was not as violent as many places in the New South. The city avoided the kind of race riots that plagued New Orleans, Atlanta, Knoxville, and Wilmington, North Carolina, during the era. Individuals such as Eartha White were able to bridge barriers in rather remarkable ways to obtain parks, health care, schools, and other assistance for the black community. Mayor Bowden reined in the police following the shootings in 1914, and many white organizations formally protested the lynchings. Clearly justice or any sense of open or equitable race relations did not prevail, but at the same time white Jacksonville did not regularly stoop to the excesses that characterized many cities and towns across the state and region. To say that, however, is small compensation to the victims of segregation, violence, and political exclusion who would see Ku Klux Klan rallies in Hemming Park during the 1920s. The New South city's greatest failure remained

Francis P. Conroy, president of the Board of Trade, 1911–1913, businessman, and civic activist. Courtesy of the Haydon Burns Library.

its retrogression in race relations during these years, and Jacksonville was no exception.[12]

Other problems arose during these years that also would affect Jacksonville well into the twentieth century. One was the consequence of rapid growth. By 1914 automobile traffic clogged downtown streets, requiring the city council to provide traffic police and legislate rules of the road. The influx of newcomers during the war overcrowded the schools, forcing double sessions. In the postwar years, public funding never caught up with educational needs. Meanwhile suburban expansion required costly public services not readily available. County roads linking Jacksonville north to Georgia, west to Lake City, and south to St. Augustine were grossly inadequate on the eve of the great Florida land boom. In sum, delayed governmental responses to changing urban needs would again become a Jacksonville characteristic.[13]

Another community concern became the increasing diversity of interests that tended to divide the city as it grew. It was seen in the conflict over the Sunday blue laws, the form of commission government, the siting of the new railroad station, the proposal to build the automobile bridge across the St. Johns River, the location of the first St. Vincent's Hospital in Springfield, the strikes, and the expansion of the city's boundaries in 1919. Conflict increasingly seemed to characterize public issues.

Meanwhile the establishment of real estate, advertising, retail, and other commercial associations meant the Chamber of Commerce no longer alone spoke for the business community. Similarly, with the growth of other women's organizations, the Woman's Club no longer spoke for middle-class white women. Despite efforts at cooperation, there surfaced a plurality of interests and a greater likelihood that such interests would conflict. Plurality of interests and conflict resolution had never been one of Jacksonville's strong suits, except in a crisis such as the fire and perhaps later in the consolidation of city with county.

Another cloud on the horizon was competition from downstate. After Flagler had built his railroad south to St. Augustine and beyond, Jacksonville's role as a tourist center had declined. Local interests continued to foster tourist development, but the city lacked the climate and amenities of Palm Beach, Coral Gables, and St. Petersburg, which already were attracting tourists and land speculators. The Florida boom of the 1920s did not entirely bypass Jacksonville, but it certainly eclipsed it as a state attraction in the popular mind. Ironically, Jacksonville money helped to fuel the boom, and the city prospered from supplying goods and services to the new resorts. Locals, torn between profiting from their role as a New South commercial center and missing the glamour of the boom, had trouble focusing on the best direction for developing their own community.[14]

Finally, as the era came to an end, the national mood began to shift from what historian Robert S. McElvaine called the cooperative individualism of the Progressive Era to the more acquisitive individualism of the 1920s. W. N. Conoley, appointed secretary to the Board of Trade in 1913, spoke to the first value in an address to the board:[15]

> The aim of every efficient body, whether called the board of trade or chamber of commerce, should be the genuine uplift of the community. . . . We may boast of our absolute independence, but the truth is, we are not. We are interdependent. Every citizen of Jacksonville owes something to the community. It is doing something for him—furnishing business and employment, friends and entertainment, schools and churches, parks and drives. . . . It re-

quires enterprise, cooperation and work to make the community a desirable city in which to live.

The president of the Woman's Club said it only slightly differently, stressing the importance of cooperation among "commercial, civic, patriotic and philanthropic organizations . . . with the state county and municipal authorities . . . working for . . . the civic betterment of the community."[16]

The success of this approach, the private-public partnership, enabled Jacksonville to become a prosperous and purposeful New South city. Its achievements would not be matched again until the generation that brought about and implemented the consolidation of Jacksonville with Duval County in the 1960s.

NOTES

Introduction

1. Henry W. Grady, "The New South" in Joel Chandler Harris, *Life of Henry W. Grady Including His Speeches and Writings* (New York: Haskell House, 1972), 83–88.

2. Ibid., 88; James M. McPherson, *Ordeal By Fire: The Civil War and Reconstruction* (New York: Knopf, 1982), esp. chap. 1; and C. Vann Woodward, *Origins of the New South, 1877–1913* (Baton Rouge: Louisiana State University Press, 1951), 150–51. See also Richard D. Brown, *Modernization: The Transformation of American Life, 1600–1865* (New York: Hill & Wang, 1976), esp. chap. 1.

3. Grady, 90.

4. Paul M. Gaston, *The New South Creed: A Study in Mythmaking* (New York: Vintage Books Edition, 1973), chap. 3, passim.

5. While glorification of the Old South also became part of the New South myth, my concerns focus on the developmental aspects. For more on both, see Gaston, chaps. 3–5; Woodward, esp. chap. 7; and George Brown Tindall, *The Emergence of the New South, 1913–1945* (Baton Rouge: Louisiana State University Press, 1967), ix, x. On Atlanta's recovery from the war, see James Michael Russell, *Atlanta, 1847–1890: City Building in the Old South and the New* (Baton Rouge: Louisiana State University Press, 1988), chap. 5. A recent study focusing on the new business class shaping the unequal development of four New South cities is Don H. Doyle, *New Men, New Cities, New South: Atlanta, Nashville, Charleston, Mobile, 1860–1910* (Chapel Hill: University of North Carolina Press, 1990).

6. Howard N. Rabinowitz, "Continuity and Change: Southern Urban Development, 1860–1900," in *The City in Southern History*, ed. Blaine A. Brownell and David R. Goldfield (Port Washington, N.Y.: Kennikat Press, 1977), 99–104; and David R. Goldfield, *Cotton Fields and Skyscrapers* (Baton Rouge; Louisiana State University Press, 1982), 92–93. An exception to this portrayal of backwardness is Doyle, *New Men, New Cities, New South.*

7. For a good discussion of the first generation of a New South city, see Russell, *Atlanta*, chap. 5. For the second generation, see Don H. Doyle, *Nashville in the New South, 1880–1930* (Knoxville: University of Tennessee Press, 1985);

Harold Platt, *City Building in the New South: The Growth of Public Services in Houston, Texas, 1830–1910* (Philadelphia: Temple University Press, 1983), chaps. 7, 8, passim.; and Carl V. Harris, *Political Power in Birmingham, 1871–1921* (Knoxville: University of Tennessee Press, 1977), esp. chap. 1. Blaine Brownell, "Birmingham, Alabama: New South City in the 1920s," *Journal of Southern History* 38 (February, 1972): 21–48, examines this theme in the years after World War I while James McGovern, "Pensacola, Florida: A Military City in the New South," *Florida Historical Quarterly* 54 (July 1980): 24–41, overlaps with this study extending through World War II.

8. Doyle, *Nashville*, and Platt, *City Building in . . . Houston*, in part address these issues.

9. Gaston, 104.

Chapter 1

1. Sanborn-Perris Map Co., Ltd., "Insurance Map of Jacksonville, Florida" (New York, 1897).

2. Ibid., and J. Wiggins and Co., *Jacksonville Directory for 1900* (Jacksonville, Fla.: author, 1900).

3. Sidney Lanier, *Florida: Its Scenery, Climate, and History* (1875; reprint, Gainesville: University of Florida Press, 1973), 67–86, passim.

4. James Esgate, *Jacksonville: The Metropolis of Florida* (Boston: W. G. M. Perry, 1885), esp. 23, 43.

5. Ibid.

6. S. Paul Brown, *The Book of Jacksonville: A History* (Poughkeepsie, N.Y.: A. V. Haight, 1893), 11, 48–49.

7. Ibid., 71–73.

8. Ibid., 135–37.

9. *Florida Times-Union and Citizen*, April 16, July 5, September 3, November 26, 27, 28, 1900, January 1, 1901 (hereafter cited as *TU&C*).

10. Ibid., February 9, 22, March 25, December 17, 1900; and Diary of Edwin Hansford Rennolds, February 21, 1900, on deposit at the P. K. Yonge Library, University of Florida.

11. *TU&C*, June 11, 1900; and U.S. Bureau of the Census, *Twelfth Census of the United States, Part II* (Washington, D.C.: U.S. Bureau of the Census, 1900), table 94, "Statistics of Population."

12. *TU&C*, November 26, 27, 28, 30, December 1, 17, 1900.

13. Ibid., November 30, December 26, 1900.

14. Charles S. Abrams, ed., *Report of the Jacksonville Auxiliary Sanitary Association of Jacksonville, Florida, Covering the Work of the Association During the Yellow Fever Epidemic, 1888* (Jacksonville, Fla., 1889), 9; Richard A. Martin, *A Century of Service: St. Luke's Hospital, 1873–1973* (Jacksonville, Fla.: n.p., 1973), 115–21; *TU&C*, January 1, 1901.

15. *TU&C*, March 23, 1900.

16. *Biennial Reports of the Superintendent of Public Instruction of the State of Florida for the Two Years Ending June 30, 1900* (Tallahassee, Fla., 1900), tables 1–8, 12; also pp. 2, 3, 22, 38, 39.

17. Barbara Ann Richardson, *A History of Blacks in Jacksonville, Florida, 1860–1895: A Socioeconomic and Political Study* (Ann Arbor, Mich.: University Microfilms, 1975), 209–20.

18. Ibid., 130–33; J. Wiggins and Co., *Jacksonville Directory for 1900*, 20–29, 319–414; J. Irving Scott, *The Education of Black People in Florida* (Philadelphia, Pa.: Dorrance, 1974), 41–43, 49–53.

19. U.S. Bureau of the Census, *Twelfth Census of the United States, Part II*, tables 89, 94; Census Bulletin no. 72, table 5.

20. *TU&C*, February 13, March 13, 24, May 15, November 27, 1900; T. Frederick Davis, *History of Jacksonville, Florida, and Vicinity, 1513–1924* (Jacksonville: Florida Historical Society, 1925), 428.

21. *Twelfth Census*, Census Bulletin no. 16, table 2; Census Bulletin no. 75, table 9; "Statistics of Population," pt. 2, table 35. For an insightful discussion of the 21 Syrians, 2 Rumanian Jews, 34 Russian Jews, 59 Italians, 111 Greeks, and 35 Chinese in Jacksonville in 1900, see Kathleen Ann Francis Cohen, "Immigrant Jacksonville: A Profile of Immigrant Groups in Jacksonville, Florida, 1890–1920" (Master's thesis, University of Florida, 1986).

22. *TU&C*, June 18, November 7, 1900.

23. Ibid., January 16, 28, February 2, 12, 27, March 13, 28, 29, 1901.

24. Davis, *History of Jacksonville*, 219–21; Benjamin Harris, *Acres of Ashes* (Jacksonville, Fla.: J. A. Holloman, 1901); *TU&C*, May 4, 1901; Charles H. Smith, *Report of the Jacksonville Relief Association* (Jacksonville, Fla., 1901).

25. *TU&C*, May 4, 1901.

26. Davis, *History of Jacksonville*, 227; *TU&C*, May 4, 6, 10, 1901; Smith, *Report of the Jacksonville Relief Association*.

Chapter 2

1. Charles H. Smith, *Report of the Jacksonville Relief Association* (Jacksonville, Fla., 1901), 7, 12, 109–10; *Florida Times-Union and Citizen*, May 5–9, 1901 (hereafter cited as *TU&C*).

2. Smith, *Report of the Jacksonville Relief Association*, 12–18. Twelve freight cars dispatched Tuesday, May 7, contained 300 men's suits, 300 boys' suits, 300 children's suits, 500 extra pair of pants, 55 pillowcases, 870 dozen women's hose, 1,110 dozen infant's hose, 700 cots, 6,000 pair of blankets, 253 dozen sheets, 515 dozen women's wrappers, 47 dozen women's shirtwaists, 928 dozen women's and children's vests, 100 dozen men's hose, 100 mattresses, and 1,088 pair of shoes. Also included were 15,900 packages of hominy, 16,000 pounds of cornmeal, 140 barrels and sacks of salt, 1,030 dozen cans of corned beef, 1,085 dozen cans of baked beans, 848 dozen cans of salmon, 26,720 packages of prepared flour, 11,920 pounds of sugar, 6,000 sides of bacon, 400 dozen cans of corn, 90 dozen cans of

pepper, 4,800 pounds of ham, 4,800 pounds of lard, 9,681 loaves of pilot bread, 370 dozen cans of soup, 1,480 dozen cans of condensed milk, 3,000 pounds of prepared codfish, 15,750 pounds of ground coffee, 56 dozen cans of mustard, 100 dozen cans of tomatoes, and 380 dozen cans of roast beef. Subsequently, six more carloads were sent containing the hoes, shovels, wheelbarrows, and sanitary water closets.

3. Ibid., 3; *TU&C*, May 4, 1901 Extra!

4. Smith, *Report of the Jacksonville Relief Association*, 4; *TU&C*, May 6, 7, 1901.

5. Smith, *Report of the Jacksonville Relief Association*, 6, 15, 21; *TU&C*, May 6, 7, 1901.

6. *TU&C*, May 5, 6, 7, 1901.

7. Ibid., May 8, 9, 1901.

8. Ibid., May 10, 11, 13, 28, 1901.

9. Ibid., May 5, 20, 1901.

10. Ibid., May 14, 18, 1901; Smith, *Report of the Jacksonville Relief Association*, 38–41, 68–72.

11. *TU&C*, May 17, 1901.

12. Ibid., May 11, 12, 17, 1901.

13. Ibid., May 16, June 20, 23, 1901.

14. Wayne Flynt, *Duncan Upshaw Fletcher: Dixie's Reluctant Progressive* (Tallahassee: Florida State University Press, 1971), chap. 1.

15. Ibid., chap. 2.

16. *TU&C*, June 19, 1901.

17. Ibid., May 23, June 8, 16, 17, July 1, 8, 19, 20, 21, December 11, 1901; and Natalie H. Glickstein, *That Ye May Remember: Congregation Ahavath Chesed, 1882–1982, 5642–5742* (St. Petersburg, Fla.: Byron Kennedy, 1982), 30.

18. Robert C. Broward, *The Architecture of Henry John Klutho: The Prairie School in Jacksonville* (Jacksonville: University of North Florida Press, 1983), chap. 1.

19. Ibid., chaps. 2–5, *passim*.

20. *TU&C*, June 2, July 5, 29, 1901.

21. Ibid., September 3, 1901.

22. Ibid., August 30, September 20, 21, 29, October 29, November 8, 1901.

23. Ibid., November 19, 20, 28, December 19, 1901.

24. James B. Crooks, "Changing Face of Jacksonville, Florida: 1900–1910," *Florida Historical Quarterly* 62 (April 1984): 444. See also John F. Stover, *The Railroads of the South, 1865–1900* (Chapel Hill: University of North Carolina Press, 1955), chap. 12.

25. Crooks, "Changing Face of Jacksonville," 444–45.

26. Jacksonville Chamber of Commerce, *Jacksonville, Florida* (Jacksonville: Arnold Printing Co., 1914), 9–12, 17–19, 33–34; *Florida Times-Union*, May 26, 1909, May 8, 1910, March 1, May 18, 1911. Beginning January 20, 1903, the newspaper dropped "and Citizen" from its masthead and became the *Florida Times-Union* (hereafter cited as *FTU*).

27. Crooks, "Changing Face of Jacksonville," 445; *FTU*, August 16, 1912.

28. Crooks, "Changing Face of Jacksonville," 445; *FTU*, August 30, 1911.

29. Afro-American Insurance Company, *Fortieth Anniversary* (Jacksonville, Fla.: n.p., 1941), 2–7; Richard A. Martin, *Images and Voices From the Past* (Jacksonville, Fla.: n.p., 1977); Clement Richardson, ed., *The National Cyclopedia of the Colored Race* (Montgomery, Ala.: National Publishing Co.), 1:463; *FTU*, October 14, 1915.

30. Richard Alan Nelson, *Florida and the American Motion Picture Industry, 1898–1930* (New York: Garland Publishing, 1983), chap. 3, esp. 163, 194.

31. Crooks, "Changing Face of Jacksonville," 442–43.

32. T. Frederick Davis, *History of Jacksonville, Florida, and Vicinity, 1513–1924* (Jacksonville: Florida Historical Society, 1925), 244–46; Crooks, "Changing Face of Jacksonville," 442; *FTU*, November 30, 1913, July 4, 1916.

33. "City of Jacksonville, Florida, Tax Data," T. Frederick Davis Papers, Box 2, P. K. Yonge Library, University of Florida; Jacksonville Chamber of Commerce, *Jacksonville, Florida* (Jacksonville, 1914), 2; *FTU*, January 1, 1901, January 1, 1914.

34. *FTU*, July 18, 19, 20, 23, 26, 29, August 2, 1902.

35. Ibid., August 3, 6, 7, 11, 12, 13, 22, September 3, October 2, 1905, January 13, 1906.

36. Ibid., October 29, 30, 31, November 1–10, 12, 15, 20, 1912.

37. Ibid., August 23, September 2, 7, 1906.

38. Ibid., July 27, 28, August 20, September 26, October 4, 1906, March 14, April 9, 21, July 11, September 12, 1907.

39. Ibid., November 11, 1907, January 3, 9, 1908.

40. Jacksonville Chamber of Commerce, *Jacksonville*, 3–52, *passim*.

41. The sample identifies 284 persons from the 1900 U.S. census manuscript and 290 persons from the 1910 U.S. census manuscript, both on microfilm at the University of North Florida Carpenter Library. Each of the city's nine wards was proportionately represented. To test the validity of the samples, I chose five sample characteristics and compared them with the published census aggregations for the

	Total sample	Total city population
1900	285 (1.0%)	28,429
Proportion blacks	164 (57.5%)	16,236 (57.1%)
Proportion whites	120 (42.1%)	12,158 (42.7%)
Proportion Asian	1 (0.3%)	35 (0.1%)
Foreign-born	14 (4.9%)	1,166 (4.1%)
Homeownership	75 of 286 (26.2%)	1,814 of 7,013 (25.9%)
1910	290 (0.5%)	57,699
Proportion blacks	145 (50.0%)	29,293 (50.8%)
Proportion whites	145 (50.0%)	28,329 (49.1%)
Proportion Asian	0 (–)	77 (0.1%)
Foreign-born	23 (7.9%)	2,688 (4.6%)
Homeownership	64 of 290 (22.1%)	3247 of 13,228 (24.5%)

entire city for the respective years. Except for a discrepancy in the number of foreign-born in the 1910 sample, the samples are representative of the entire city population.

See also R. Christian Johnson, "A Procedure for Sampling the Mss. Census Schedules," *Journal of Interdisciplinary History* 8 (1978): 515–30.

42. The classification system comes from Stephan Thernstrom, *The Other Bostonians: Poverty and Progress in the American Metropolis, 1880–1970* (Cambridge, Mass.: Harvard University Press, 1973), appendix B, 289–392, esp. table B.1.

> *I. High White Collar* occupations at the turn of the century included architect, clergy, editor, lawyer, pharmacist, physician, teacher, and other clearly professional people, plus major proprietors, managers, and officials of banks, brokers, large contractors, corporation officials, manufacturers, hotel keepers or managers, substantial merchants, and upper-level government officials.
>
> *II. Low White Collar* occupations included bank teller, bookkeeper, clerk, salesperson, secretary or typist, actor, artist, chiropractor, journalist, musician, writer, foreman, minor government official, proprietor or manager of a small business, and self-employed artisan.
>
> *III. Skilled Blue Collar* occupations included baker, locksmith, boilermaker, bricklayer, mason, carpenter, locomotive engineer, jeweler, machinist, millwright, painter, paperhanger, plasterer, plumber, tailor, trimmer, etc.
>
> *IV. Semiskilled and Service Worker* occupations include barber, bartender, chauffeur, cook, firefighter, policeman, janitor, longshoreman, milkman, soldier or sailor (enlisted), servant or stevedore, fisherman, guard, hospital attendant, teamster, waiter, or welder.
>
> *V. Unskilled* occupations include gardener, liveryman, laborer, and porter.

43. Data on women in Jacksonville are less complete. The survey focused on heads of households, who were mostly men. Yet the sample for 1900 included sixty-one women. Two-thirds of these women worked in semiskilled or menial jobs and almost all were black, an early feminization of poverty. African-American women comprised 80 percent of the female heads of household sample and one-third of the black heads of household. The 1910 sample included fewer women (fifty-eight) and is less open to speculative generalization. Still, most women held blue-collar jobs; 62 percent were black.

44. James Weldon Johnson, *Along This Way* (New York: Viking Press, 1933), 45.

45. The comparisons come from Howard P. Chudacoff and Judith E. Smith, *The Evolution of American Urban Society*, 3d ed. (Englewood Cliffs, N.J.: Prentice-Hall, 1988), 141.

46. Thernstrom, *Other Bostonians*, 232–41, puts a more positive emphasis on the 10 to 20 percent of urban Americans who had substantial upward occupational mobility during their lifetimes in these years, perhaps because of the more

negative emphasis of his earlier study, *Poverty and Progress: Social Mobility in a Nineteenth Century City* (New York: Atheneum, 1964).

47. The quote is from Chudacoff and Smith, *Evolution of American Urban Society*, 142–43. Howard P. Chudacoff, *Mobile Americans: Residential and Social Mobility in Omaha, 1880–1920* (New York: Oxford University Press, 1972), 154–57, describes comparable residential mobility except for black Americans confined to particular neighborhoods. See also Thernstrom, *Other Bostonians*, esp. chap. 9. The persistence rate for Jacksonville from 1900 to 1914 was 42 percent (86 of 207), which was roughly comparable to other cities in Thernstrom's studies (table 9.1, 222). I go beyond persistence in the community, however, when I suggest a greater restlessness (90 percent) that raises questions about one's home as castle or place of refuge. See also Peter R. Knights, *The Plain People of Boston, 1830–1860* (New York: Oxford University Press, 1971), esp. chap. 4.

48. Davis, *History of Jacksonville*, 250–52; *FTU*, July 9, 1915, January 1, 1916, January 29, 1917.

49. Davis, *History of Jacksonville*, 251; *FTU*, January 1, 1916.

50. *FTU*, December 16, 1914, June 20, 1915.

51. Ibid., November 4, December 8, 1914, January 27, October 22, 1915; July 3, 1916.

52. Jacksonville Board of Trade, *Address of the President and Annual Reports of the Secretary and Treasurer for the Year Ending, November 30, 1914* (Jacksonville, Fla., 1915), 7; *FTU*, June 19, 1915.

53. Jerrell H. Shofner, "Florida and the Black Migration," *Florida Historical Quarterly* 57 (January 1979): 267–68.

54. *FTU*, July 3, September 12, 1916, March 24, November 6, 1917.

Chapter 3

1. *Constitution of the State of Florida: Adopted at the Convention of 1885 and Ratified by the People at the Election of November 2, 1886* (Tallahassee, Fla., 1886), article 8, sect. 8.

2. T. Frederick Davis, *History of Jacksonville, Florida, and Vicinity, 1513–1924* (Jacksonville: Florida Historical Society, 1925), 287–91.

3. Wayne Flynt, *Duncan Upshaw Fletcher: Dixie's Reluctant Progressive* (Tallahassee: Florida State University Press, 1971), 11–20; Edwin N. Akin, "When a Minority Becomes a Majority: Blacks in Jacksonville Politics, 1877–1907," *Florida Historical Quarterly* 53 (October 1974): 130–36. In 1892, of 2,365 Jacksonvillians who paid the poll tax, only 137 were black (Flynt, 27).

4. James B. Crooks, "Jacksonville in the Progressive Era: Responses to Urban Growth" *Florida Historical Quarterly* 65 (July 1986): 65–66; *Florida Times-Union*, July 1, 1911 (hereafter cited as *FTU*). The Board of Bond Trustees was a popular abbreviation for its legal title, the Board of Trustees for the Waterworks and Improvement Bonds of the City of Jacksonville, Florida. Jon C. Teaford, *The Un-*

heralded Triumph: City Government in America, 1870–1900 (Baltimore, Md.: Johns Hopkins University Press, 1984), 66–80, addresses the issue of appointed boards and commissions similar to the one in Jacksonville during these years.

5. Crooks, 66–67.

6. *FTU*, August 21, 23, 26, 28, October 19, 25, 1913, August 22, September 6, October 11, 1914, May 29, September 8, 1915.

7. Ibid., April 16, 1901, May 24, 1905, April 6, 1907. See also David R. Colburn and Richard K. Scher, *Florida's Gubernatorial Politics in the Twentieth Century* (Tallahassee: Florida State University Press, 1980), esp. part 3.

8. *FTU*, March 11, 1914, April 21, 1915.

9. *Tenth Annual Report of the Railroad Commission of the State of Florida for the Year Ending March 1, 1907* (Jacksonville: The Commission, 1907), 4–7; *Eleventh Annual Report of the Railroad Commission of the State of Florida for the Year Ending March 1, 1908* (Jacksonville: The Commission, 1908), 5.

10. *Railroad Commission Minute Book*, series 205, col. 5, January 27, 1913, on deposit at the Florida State Archives; *FTU*, February 19, 1912.

11. *The State of Florida ex rel.* vs. *Jacksonville Terminal Company, et al., Cases Adjudicated in the Supreme Court of Florida, During the January Term, 1916* 71 (Deland, Fla., 1916), 295–338.

12. Ibid.; *FTU*, August 18, 1915, November 17, 1919.

13. Crooks, "Jacksonville in the Progressive Era," 60; Linda Emerson Sabin, "Nursing and Health Care in Jacksonville, Florida, 1900–1930" (Master's thesis, University of Florida, 1988), 21–22, 58.

14. Crooks, "Jacksonville in the Progressive Era," 62.

15. Ibid.

16. Sabin, "Nursing and Health Care," 58; *FTU*, January 1, 1904, June 28, 1910.

17. David T. Courtwright, "Charles Terry, *The Opium Problem*, and American Narcotic Policy," *Journal of Drug Issues* 16 (1983): 423; *FTU*, July 14, December 14, 1916.

18. *FTU*, May 15, 17, 18, September 5, 1910.

19. City of Jacksonville, Florida, *Annual Report of the Board of Health for the Year 1911* (Jacksonville, 1912), 47.

20. Ibid., 1910, 10; see also *FTU*, June 28, September 5, 1910.

21. City of Jacksonville, *Annual Report of the Board of Health, 1916*, 29.

22. Edward R. Smith, M.D., "Seven Years of Pioneering in Preventive Medicine," *Journal of the Florida Medical Association* 53 (August 1966): 725–28. See also City of Jacksonville, *Annual Reports, passim*.

23. City of Jacksonville, *Annual Report of the Board of Health 1913*, 22.

24. Ibid., 25.

25. Ibid., 1916, 26.

26. Ibid., 1912, 24–26.

27. Ibid., 1914, 25–29. Both morphine and laudanum are opium derivatives

used to relieve pain. Morphine is an alkaloid, while laudanum is opium in a camphorated tincture.

28. David T. Courtwright, "The Hidden Epidemic: Opiate Addiction and Cocaine Use in the South, 1860–1920," *Journal of Southern History* 49 (February 1983): 67–68; and City of Jacksonville, *Annual Report of the Board of Health, 1914*, 27.

29. City of Jacksonville, *Annual Report of the Board of Health, 1913*, 28; ibid., 1915, 47.

30. Both black and white rates were down, with the black rate declining further from 25.3 to 18.4 per thousand and the white rate from 15.9 to 12.9 per thousand. Courtwright, "Charles Terry," 426; City of Jacksonville, *Annual Report of the Board of Health, 1916*, 11–12, 118. Terry later coauthored, with Mildred Pellens, a massive, landmark study of drugs, *The Opium Problem* (Montclair, N.J.: Patterson Smith, 1970 reprint).

31. Terry & Pellens, *The Opium Problem*, 14.

32. Ibid., 37–38.

33. Ibid., 21–23, 40–41.

34. Ibid., 30–31.

35. Ibid., 42–44. *FTU*, May 30, 1916, claimed Jacksonville's per-capita expenditure for public health was the highest for any southern city with over 30,000 population.

36. *Biennial Report of the Superintendent of Public Instruction of the State of Florida for the Two Years Ending June 30, 1900* (Tallahassee, 1900), 275; *FTU*, February 2, 1900.

37. Crooks, "Jacksonville in the Progressive Era," 56; Minutes of the Board of Public Instruction of Duval County, Florida, May 17, September 21, 1901 (hereafter referred to as School Board Minutes); *FTU*, March 26, 1903.

38. *FTU*, February 8, April 3, 18, 25, 1903, October 21, 1907.

39. *Biennial Report*, 1900; ibid., 1910; School Board Minutes, January 5, 1906.

40. School Board Minutes, September 20, 1906, March 7, December 6, 1907, January 28, 1908, January 23, 1909, November 4, 1911.

41. Ibid., November 28, December 18, 1909, May 6, 1911, April 6, May 1, June 1, 1912. Per-pupil expenditure and enrollment figures can be found in the *Biennial Report* for the appropriate year.

42. *FTU*, May 13, October 6, 1910, May 6, 1911; School Board Minutes, April 30, May 28, October 8, 1910.

43. Crooks, "Jacksonville in the Progressive Era," 58.

44. Ibid., 58–59.

45. Ibid., 59.

46. *Biennial Report*, 1914, 523–27; ibid., 1916, 608–18; ibid., 1918, 592; School Board Minutes, February 20, 1915.

47. Quoted in *FTU*, June 24, 1916.

48. *Biennial Report*, 1918; *FTU*, November 9, 1918.

49. Courtwright, "Charles Terry," 422–25; Daniel P. Gold, *History of Duval County, Including Early History of East Florida* (St. Augustine, Fla.: Record Co., 1929), 539. See also Teaford, *Unheralded Triumph*, chap. 6, for a discussion of the role of the urban professional beginning in the Gilded Age.

50. Crooks, "Jacksonville in the Progressive Era," 53–56.

51. Flynt, *Fletcher*, 30–40.

52. *FTU*, June 25, 26, July 12, 1913.

53. Ibid., August 9, 1913, May 4, 13, 1914.

54. Ibid., May 15, 30, October 24, 1914, January 31, February 6, 10, 11, 12, 21, 23, 24, 1915; Wayne Flynt, *Cracker Messiah: Governor Sidney J. Catts of Florida* (Baton Rouge: Louisiana State University Press, 1977), 101.

55. *FTU*, June 25, August 1, September 7, 29, 1915, January 12, July 30, 1916; Richard Alan Nelson, *Florida and the American Motion Picture Industry, 1898–1980*, 2 vols. (New York: Garland, 1983), 162–65, 177–78, 180–84, 224.

56. *Report of the Chief of Engineers, U.S. Army, 1914* (Washington, D.C.: Government Printing Office, 1914), 631–632; George E. Buker, *Sun, Sand and Water: A History of the Jacksonville District, U.S. Army Corps of Engineers, 1821–1975* (Fort Belvoir, Va.: U.S. Army Corps of Engineers, 1981), 69–83.

57. U.S. House of Representatives, 2d sess., "St. Johns River, Florida," *Report to the Committee on Rivers and Harbors*, Document no. 611, January 29, 1910, 3–22, *passim*.

58. *FTU*, May 29, June 21, July 13, August 20, 1912; correspondence from Duncan U. Fletcher to General Dan C. Kingman, Chief of Engineers, Records Group 77, National Archives. While Senator Fletcher's correspondence and the *FTU* show that the War Department/Corps of Engineers required Jacksonville to build the municipal docks, there is no clear indication why. One source claims that Claude L'Engle, itinerate journalist, politician, reformer, gadfly, and racist, first lobbied for them, and that George R. Spaulding heard, agreed, and issued an ultimatum that no further funds would be spent by the War Department until municipal docks were built (Claude L'Engle Papers, P. K. Yonge Library, University of Florida).

59. *FTU*, May 29, August 18, 19, October 11, 1912, January 23, 1913.

Chapter 4

1. Alexis de Tocqueville, *Democracy in America*, ed. J. P. Mayer, trans. George Lawrence (New York: Anchor Books, 1969), 513.

2. Charles H. Smith, "The Jacksonville Board of Trade," in S. Paul Brown, *The Book of Jacksonville, a History* (Poughkeepsie, N.Y., 1895), 69–70.

3. Ibid., 70–71.

4. Ibid., 71.

5. Richard H. Edmonds, "Spirit of the South at Jacksonville," *Manufacturer's*

Record, May 23, 1903, quoted in Jacksonville Board of Trade, *Report for 1903–1904* (Jacksonville, Fla., 1904), 12.

6. Ibid.

7. *Florida Times-Union*, January 16, 1904, April 28, 1905, July 26–October 4, 1906, *passim*, March 14–April 9, April 21, July 11, September 12, 1907 (hereafter cited as *FTU*).

8. Charles H. Smith, "Jacksonville and Florida Facts" prepared for the Jacksonville Board of Trade (Jacksonville, 1906), 39.

9. *FTU*, May 13, 1910, January 5, 1911, August 22, 1920; Jacksonville Board of Trade, *Reports of the President and Secretary-Treasurer for the Year Ending December 31, 1909* (Jacksonville, Fla., 1910).

10. Jacksonville Board of Trade, *Reports, 1910* (Jacksonville, Fla., 1911); *FTU*, May 29, June 21, August 18, 1912, January 23, 1913.

11. *FTU*, March 5, 1912, July 19, September 6, 9, 12, 1913; Jacksonville Board of Trade, *Reports, 1912* (Jacksonville, Fla., 1913); and ibid., 1913 (Jacksonville, Fla., 1914).

12. Jacksonville Chamber of Commerce, *Jacksonville Today* (Jacksonville, 1915), also stressed Duval County's agricultural potential. The chamber established an agricultural and market bureau in cooperation with the U.S. Department of Agriculture with twenty-five demonstration farms scattered across Duval County. See also David R. Goldfield, *Cotton Fields and Skyscrapers: Southern City and Region, 1607–1980* (Baton Rouge: Louisiana State University Press, 1982), 3–4, for another view of southern cities maintaining strong ties with their agricultural hinterlands.

The black community, of course, benefited much less than the white community, though parks, schools, entertainment, and public health programs with their benefits did reach many of its members. The working class also benefited, though to a substantially lesser extent than prosperous business owners and managers. Women, depending on their roles, benefited at different levels, but almost always less than men of their same class, race, or ethnic group.

13. Jacksonville Board of Trade, *Address of the President and Annual Reports of Secretary and Treasurer for the Year Ending November 30, 1914* (Jacksonville, Fla., 1915), 7; and Jacksonville Chamber of Commerce, *Address of the President and Annual Reports of Secretary and Treasurer for the Year Ending November 30, 1915* (Jacksonville, Fla., 1916), 7.

14. *FTU*, July 8, December 30, 1915. See also the annual reports for member counts.

15. *FTU*, July 15, August 7, 1915.

16. Ibid., April 6–27, 1916.

17. Ibid., May 11, 1911.

18. Anne Firor Scott, *The Southern Lady: From Pedestal to Politics, 1830–1930* (Chicago: University of Chicago Press, 1970), chap. 6, esp. p. 158.

19. Woman's Club of Jacksonville, *Annual Report, 1905–1906* (Jacksonville, Fla., 1906), 29.

20. Paul Gaston, *The New South Creed: A Study in Southern Mythmaking* (New York: Knopf, 1970), 103–4.

21. *FTU*, April 3, 1903, May 23, 1912.

22. Ibid., April 8, 25, 1903, February 8, 1905.

23. Ibid., June 7, 1902.

24. Ibid., November 21, 23, 1905.

25. Linda D. Vance, *May Mann Jennings: Florida's Genteel Activist* (Gainesville: University of Florida Press, 1985), 140. See also the May Mann Jennings Papers on deposit at the P. K. Yonge Library, University of Florida, esp. boxes 3, 4, 5.

26. Ibid., chaps. 1–3, *passim*.

27. Woman's Club of Jacksonville, *Annual Report, 1909–1910*, 35–39; *Annual Report, 1912–1913*, 42. See the May Mann Jennings Papers, box 4, for the text of one of her lectures to a political science class on the problems of the city.

28. Woman's Club of Jacksonville, *Annual Report, 1908–1909*, 48; *Annual Report, 1911–1912*, 51; *Annual Report, 1912–1913*, 50; *FTU*, May 5, June 3, October 15, 1908, January 18, 28, February 5, May 29, 1909, November 27, 1910, May 7, 1911.

29. *First Annual Report of the Associated Charities, Jacksonville, Florida, March 16–December 31, 1910* (Jacksonville, 1911), 7–11; *FTU*, February 8, 1907, June 7, October 12, 27, 31, November 5, December 9, 1909, January 18, 1910.

30. *First Annual Report of Associated Charities*, 11.

31. The authorization of Royal Palm State Park by the legislature in 1915 was the first step toward the eventual creation of Everglades National Park by the federal government in 1947. See Vance, *May Mann Jennings*, 80–86, 129–32.

32. Woman's Club of Jacksonville, *Annual Report, 1910–1911*, 40–45, describes the departments. Additional data are taken from annual reports from the following years up to 1916. See also *FTU*, January 15, 17, April 11, July 16, 1911, February 9, May 23, 1912.

33. Woman's Club of Jacksonville, *Annual Report, 1911–1912*, 44.

34. Ibid., 1912–1913, 47.

35. Ibid., 1913–1914, 39, and 1914–1915, 44.

36. Vance, *May Mann Jennings*, 69; "Report of Jail Committee," box 3, May Mann Jennings Papers.

37. Woman's Club of Jacksonville, *Annual Report, 1915–1916*, 39. See also *FTU*, May 21, 1916; letter from May Mann Jennings to Mary McLeod Bethune, July 20, 1917, box 11 of the Jennings Papers, where she wrote of Miss White, "She is an exceedingly bright and energetic woman, and seems never to be weary of doing well. . . . You may be assured wherever it is possible for me to assist the colored women of Florida, it will be a great pleasure for me to do so."

38. Vance, *May Mann Jennings*, 70; and Pleasant Daniel Gold, *History of Duval County, Florida*, (St. Augustine, Fla.: The Record Co., 1928), 282.

39. Conroy was quoted in *Annual Report, 1910–1911*, 39.

40. Louis R. Harlan, *Booker T. Washington: The Making of a Black Leader, 1856–1901* (New York: Oxford University Press, 1972).

41. The Jacksonville city directory for 1900 did not distinguish between African Methodist Episcopal, Methodist Episcopal, and other Methodist churches; in fact, over the years, mistaken identification was common.

42. *FTU*, October 15, 1988 (a special edition celebrating the sesquicentennial of Bethel); for the regional perspective, see Eric Foner, *Reconstruction: America's Unfinished Revolution, 1863–1877* (New York: Harper & Row, 1988), 88–93.

43. Louis R. Harlan et al., eds., *The Booker T. Washington Papers* (Urbana: University of Illinois Press, 1980), 9: 277; *FTU*, October 15, 1988.

44. *Florida Daily Sun*, December 24, 1904; "History and Souvenir of Bethel Baptist Institutional Church" (1931), found in folder F of the Eartha M. M. White Papers on deposit at the University of North Florida Library; Barbara Ann Richardson, *A History of Blacks in Jacksonville, Florida, 1860–1895: A Socioeconomic and Political Study* (Ann Arbor, Mich.: University Microfilms, 1975), 176–77.

45. "Fortieth Anniversary of the Afro-American Life Insurance Company, 1901–1941," on deposit in folder B of the White Papers, University of North Florida.

46. *FTU*, October 22, 1905; Jacksonville *Metropolis*, October 23, 1905.

47. Harlan et al., eds., *Washington Papers* 9: 277. Waldron served on the Executive Committee of the original NAACP.

48. Clement Richardson, ed., *The National Cyclopedia of the Colored Race* (Montgomery, Ala.: National Publishing Co., 1919), 1:472.

49. Daniel L. Schafer, "Eartha M. M. White: The Early Years of a Jacksonville Humanitarian" (Typescript, 1976), 22.

50. White Papers, particularly folder Z-2; *FTU*, April 14, 1910. See also Cynthia Neverdon-Morton, *Afro-American Women of the South and the Advancement of the Race, 1895–1925* (Knoxville: University of Tennessee Press, 1989); she describes the development of the National Association of Colored Women with particular emphasis on the southern cities of Baltimore, Hampton, Tuskegee, and Atlanta. White was doubtless a member of this group as was her friend, Mary McLeod Bethune.

51. *FTU*, April 25, September 29, October 4, 1901, November 7, 1909, November 3, 4, 1913. See also White Papers, folder M-1; R. R. Wright, ed. and comp., *Encyclopedia of African Methodism* (Philadelphia, Pa., n.p., 1947), 122; Wayne W. Wood, *Jacksonville's Architectural Heritage: Landmarks for the Future* (Jacksonville: University of North Florida Press, 1989), 8, 359.

52. *FTU*, February 12, 1905.

53. Jervis Anderson, *A. Philip Randolph, a Biographical Portrait* (New York: Harcourt Brace Jovanovich, 1973), 44–52.

54. Eugene Levy, *James Weldon Johnson, Black Leader, Black Voice* (Chicago: University of Chicago Press, 1973), chaps. 1–3.

55. Ibid.; and James Weldon Johnson, *Along This Way: The Autobiography of James Weldon Johnson* (reprint; New York: Da Capo Press, 1973), chap. 12.

56. Linda Emerson Sabin, "Nursing and Health Care in Jacksonville, Florida, 1900–1930" (Master's thesis, University of Florida, 1988), 68–73.

57. Harlan et al., eds., *Washington Papers* 11: 482.

58. J. Wiggins and Co., *Jacksonville Directory for 1900* (Jacksonville: author, 1900); R. L. Polk and Co., *Jacksonville City Directory, 1915* (Jacksonville: author, 1915).

59. Ibid.

60. Jerrell H. Shofner, "Florida and the Black Migration," *Florida Historical Quarterly* 58 (January 1979): 267–68.

61. Ibid., 269–71; *FTU*, July 13, August 6, 8, 18, 1916.

62. *FTU*, August 18, 1916.

63. Edward N. Akin, "When a Minority Becomes the Majority: Blacks in Jacksonville Politics, 1887–1907," *Florida Historical Quarterly* 53 (October 1974): 123–45. See also Peter D. Klingman, *Neither Dies nor Surrenders: A History of the Republican Party in Florida, 1867–1970*, (Gainesville: University of Florida Press, 1984), chaps. 6–8.

64. Richardson, *A History of Blacks in Jacksonville*, 206–20; and James B. Crooks, "Jacksonville in the Progressive Era: Responses to Urban Growth," *Florida Historical Quarterly* 65 (July 1986): 68–69.

65. *FTU*, October 28, 1906, May 10, 1908.

Chapter 5

1. Gunther Barth, *City People: The Rise of Modern City Culture in Nineteenth-Century America* (New York: Oxford University Press, 1980), 25.

2. I have omitted a discussion of apartment houses in Jacksonville. Though some were built in this era, their impact on urban life was much less than in northern cities.

Perhaps to the surprise of the modern reader, the *Florida Times-Union* was a metropolitan newspaper with probably the widest readership in the state during the early years of the twentieth century.

Though the Ostrich Farm existed as a kind of amusement park before the turn of the century, its main attraction was for tourists and it lacked the diversity of attractions that it would develop after the fire.

3. David R. Goldfield, *Cotton Fields and Skyscrapers: Southern City and Region, 1607–1980* (Baton Rouge: Louisiana State University Press, 1982), 1–11; Ted Ownby, "Evangelicalism and Male Culture: Recreation and Religion in the Rural South, 1865–1920" (Ph.D. diss., Johns Hopkins University, 1986), esp. chap. 1.

4. *Florida Times-Union*, January 6, 1909, December 26, 1915 (hereafter cited as *FTU*). These statements reflect my reading of particularly the *FTU* daily from 1900 to 1919.

5. George Mowry in the first edition of *The Urban Nation* (New York: Hill and Wang, 1965), chap. 1, suggested that the 1920s saw the rise of the mass-production-consumption society. But see also Richard W. Fox and T. J. Jackson Lears, eds., *The Culture of Consumption: Critical Essays in American History, 1880–1980* (New York: Pantheon Books, 1987); Daniel Horowitz, *The Morality of Spending: Attitudes toward the Consumer Society in America, 1875–1940* (Baltimore, Md.: Johns Hopkins University Press, 1985).

6. *FTU*, September 27, 1913, for a sample column of "News of Interest among the Colored People"; see Frank Luther Mott, *American Journalism* (New York: Macmillan Co., 1941), chaps. 26 and 31, for discussions of the new journalism.

7. Barth, *City People*, chap. 4, esp. p. 111.

8. *FTU*, October 22, 1912; Robert C. Broward, *The Architecture of Henry John Klutho* (Jacksonville: University of North Florida Press, 1983), esp. chap. 3.

9. *FTU*, April 2, 1916.

10. Barth, *City People*, chap. 5, for the ballpark's impact in northern cities.

11. Steven A. Riess, *Touching Base: Professional Baseball and American Culture in the Progressive Era* (Westport, Conn.: Greenwood Press, 1980), 112. *FTU*, February 6, March 19, 1903, March 10, 1905, March 19, 1906, February 25, 1908, February 28, 1914, March 7, 1915, March 10, 1916, and March 12, 1917.

12. Ibid., July 5, 6, 1910.

13. On black sports, see *FTU*, June 11, 1910, September 1, 1912, September 27, November 3, 9, 1913, and November 4, 5, 1915, and *The Metropolis*, March 29, 1907. For girls' basketball, see *FTU*, January 30, March 14, 1913. For Duval High School boys' sports, see ibid., December 13, 1908, February 13, 1909, December 8, 1912. Reminiscences about Randolph can be found in Jervis Anderson, *A. Philip Randolph, A Biographical Portrait* (New York: Harcourt Brace Jovanovich, 1972), 46.

14. Dale A. Somers, *The Rise of Sports in New Orleans, 1850–1900* (Baton Rouge: Louisiana State University Press, 1972), 275.

15. On Jacksonville theaters, see *Souvenir and Tourist Guide of Jacksonville, Florida* (Jacksonville, n.p., 1910); *FTU*, October 10, 1908, June 22, 1911. On films, *see* ibid., March 2, 1906. On personal appearances, for Ethel Barrymore, ibid., January 12, 1915, January 12, 1917; on Sarah Bernhardt, ibid., March 17, 1906, January 14, 1917. On black theaters, see ibid., September 1, 1912, November 2, 9, 1913. For an extended discussion of Jacksonville's history in the motion picture industry during these years, see Richard Alan Nelson, *Florida and the American Motion Picture Industry, 1898–1980* (New York: Garland, 1983), chap. 3.

16. Robert Sklar, *Movie-Made America: A Cultural History of American Movies* (New York: Random House, 1975), 89–90.

17. Joel Williamson, *The Crucible of Race: Black-White Relations in the American South since Emancipation* (New York: Oxford University Press, 1984), 140, 175–76.

18. *FTU*, April 20, 1903, November 26, 1908, December 4, 1910, Septem-

ber 29, 1911, January 6, 1912, November 7, 1916. See also *The Metropolis*, March 8, 1907.

19. On Phoenix Park, see *FTU*, July 6, 1901, July 7, August 14, 1902, April 12, 1903, April 8, 1904. On Dixieland Amusement Park, see Seaboard Air Line Railway, *Mercantile and Industrial Review of Jacksonville Florida* (Portsmouth, Va.: n.p., 1906); *FTU*, March 10, April 9, 1907, January 27, April 6, July 9, 1908, August 25, 1909, January 7, 1910, August 15, 1911, October 7, 1916. For Lincoln Park, see ibid., September 28, 1903, August 17, 1904, March 21, 1906, February 3, 1907, March 21, 1909, June 11, 1910, and *The Metropolis*, February 2, March 16, 1907. For Mason Park, see *FTU*, August 22, 1903, January 2, 1904, November 24, 1907, March 22, 1908.

20. John F. Kasson, *Amusing the Millions: Coney Island at the Turn of the Century* (New York: Hill and Wang, 1978), 41–42, 50.

21. *FTU*, March 13, June 2, 1900.

22. Ibid., August 27, 1901, June 4, 1904, February 26, 1911, March 20, May 21, 1912, July 5, 1913, July 4, 1915, July 1, 1916.

23. Ibid., July 3, 1903, May 15, 1905, June 18, July 5, 1906, April 12, May 26, 1911, June 5, 1914, June 13, 1915. For Palmetto Lodge, see Lillian Gilkes, *Cora Crane: A Biography of Mrs. Stephen Crane* (Bloomington: Indiana University Press, 1960), chap. 8.

24. *FTU*, October 7, 1906, July 29, 1910, September 1, 1912. Part of Manhattan Beach was purchased by the navy at the beginning of World War II to establish the Mayport Naval Base. Blacks then moved north of the St. Johns River to establish another resort at American Beach on Amelia Island in Nassau County, Florida.

25. Stephen Hardy, *How Boston Played: Sport, Recreation and Community, 1864–1915* (Boston, Mass.: Northeastern University Press, 1982), 15, 190–200.

26. Mencken is quoted in James R. Ward, *Old Hickory's Town: An Illustrated History of Jacksonville* (Jacksonville: Florida Publishing Co., 1982), 186.

27. Seaboard Air Line Railway, *Mercantile and Industrial Review of Jacksonville Florida*; and R. L. Polk & Co., *Jacksonville City Directory, 1915*. The observations about the various types of religious activities result from my reading the daily newspaper from 1900 to 1920, and Kathleen Ann Francis Cohen, "Immigrant Jacksonville: A Profile of Immigrant Groups in Jacksonville, Florida, 1890–1920" (Master's thesis, University of Florida, 1986).

28. *FTU*, November 14, 22, December 12, 1904, January 19, 21, 23, 25, 30, February 6, 7, March 6, 1905.

29. Ownby, "Evangelicalism and Male Culture: Recreation and Religions in the Rural South, 1865–1920," esp. chap. 6. Attitudes toward recreation were also complicated by the double standard of the era by which women were considered vessels of sanctity and men too often bestial or immoral in their behavior. Ownby describes this division in the rural South, and of course many rural southerners migrated to Jacksonville during these years. Still, in Jacksonville, the division was

not complete. Many men there, not just the clergy but leaders in business and the professions, played major roles in social reforms.

30. *FTU*, September 27, 1901, March 23, 1903, July 7, 1904, June 8, 15, October 28, 1905.

31. Ibid., December 15, 16, 20, 22, 23, 1909, January 25, February 7, March 7, 1912.

32. Ibid., February 24, March 22, 1910, April 8–May 6, May 14, 1911.

33. Ibid., February 14, 1908. For more about Cora Crane's house, see Gilkes, *Cora Crane*, esp. chap. 8.

34. *FTU*, February 12, 19, 20, 23, 26 and September 23, 1912, February 25, May 4, 13, 14, 15, 30, 1914.

35. Ibid., August 20, 21, 24, 29, September 3, 7, November 8, 16, 1907.

36. Businessmen in the hotel, restaurant, or entertainment trade tended to be wet along with men engaged directly in the manufacture or sale of alcoholic beverages. Germans, Irish, Catholics, Lutherans, and Episcopalians tended to be wet. People of Scottish or English descent, Baptists, Methodists, and Presbyterians tended to be dry. Ibid., August 20, September 27, October 5, 24, 27, 30, November 4, 9, 16, 17, 1907, February 22, 1908.

37. Ibid., February 10, 12, 14, 15, 1908.

38. Ibid., October 16, 24, 25, November 6, 8, 10, 1910.

39. Ibid., March 22, 1911, April 30, May 23, October 1, 1915, March 4, 1916.

40. Ibid., December 3, 1901, July 15, 1905, October 12, 17, 31, November 11, 1909, September 11, 1907.

41. Dewey W. Grantham, *Southern Progressivism: The Reconciliation of Progress and Tradition* (Knoxville: University of Tennessee Press, 1983), 15–25, examines the church's participation in the Social Gospel across the region.

Chapter 6

1. In chapter 2, I discussed the economic depression in Jacksonville resulting from the European war. An estimated 4,000 to 5,000 vacant houses resulted from the depression, according to the *Florida Times-Union*, May 25, 1919 (hereafter cited as *FTU*). In chapter 5 I discussed black migration. See Woman's Club of Jacksonville, "Annual Report, 1916–1917," 48, on the relief efforts.

2. *FTU*, March 24, 25, 27, 1917.

3. Ibid., April 22, 27, June 30, 1917.

4. Ibid., April 1, 26, 27, May 9, 27, June 20, July 11, 14, August 18, 1917.

5. Duncan U. Fletcher to Hon. Newton D. Baker, June 22, 1916, and Williams J. Sears to Hon. Newton D. Baker, June 21, 1917, on deposit in the Office of the Adjutant General (AGO) Document File, Record Group 94, Box 8291, File 2416708. Duncan U. Fletcher to Hon. Newton D. Baker, June 28, 1917; Newton D. Baker to General Leonard Wood, May 28, 1917; Newton D. Baker to Sen. Duncan U. Fletcher, July 12, 1917, all in AGO, Box 8971 and File 2593945, on deposit in the National Archives, Washington, D.C. See T. Frederick Davis,

History of Jacksonville, Florida and Vicinity, 1513–1924 (Jacksonville: Florida Historical Society, 1925), 262–66. Davis suggests (263), that "on account of military reasons involving the I.W.W. [International Workers of the World] in certain sections, the camp-site had been changed from Jacksonville," but Baker's letter makes reference only to "military strategic reasons."

6. June 26, 1917. A copy of this letter can be found in Raymond B. Fosdick to Mrs. W. S. Jennings, July 26, 1917, May Mann Jennings Papers, P. K. Yonge Library, University of Florida, Box 11.

7. May Mann Jennings to Hon. Raymond D. [*sic*] Fosdick, October 19, 1917, Jennings Papers, Box 13. See also *FTU*, October 14, 1917.

8. *FTU*, January 15, 18, February 23, 1918.

9. Ibid., January 8, 15, May 6, 7, 10, 15, 1918.

10. Ibid., May 15, 1918; Russell Mott to Morale Officer, Camp J. E. Johnston, December 12, 1918, and Russell Mott to Chief, Morale Branch, Washington, D.C., November 29, 1918, Record Group 165, National Archives. Mott also reported that a number of the plainclothesmen of the Military Police also were operating with the illegal liquor sellers in Jacksonville. Their method was to rob by force on the highway an illegal liquor seller transporting liquor and then sell it through their friends, dividing the proceeds. "Two days of sweating of the guilty parties broke one of them down and [he] confessed that in one case they gave the head of the Police Division in camp eighteen quarts of whiskey as his share" (Mott memo dated November 29, 1918).

11. *FTU*, May 10, 15, 30, 1917.

12. Ibid., September 21, October 7, 29, December 16, 1917, January 20, 1918; Davis, *History of Jacksonville*, 270.

13. *FTU*, January 3, April 3, 7, July 5, 1918; City Council Minute Book, April 5, 1918; Linda D. Vance, *May Mann Jennings, Florida's Genteel Activist* (Gainesville: University of Florida Press, 1985), 104; and Clement Richardson, ed., *The National Cyclopedia of the Colored Race* (Montgomery, Ala.: National Publishing Co., 1919), 470.

14. Ibid., November 9, December 8, 26, 1917, April 15, 1918; Vance, *May Mann Jennings*, 102; Edith Gray (Mrs. Leonard) Wallis, "The History of the Jacksonville (Florida), Chapter, American Red Cross, March 20, 1914 to November 16, 1920, World War I Period" (Typescript on deposit at the Haydon Burns Library, Jacksonville), 3, 22; William J. Breen, "Black Women and the Great War; Mobilization and Reform in the South" *Journal of Southern History* 44 (August 1978): 430, 437, 439.

15. Report of Merrill Stevens Shipbuilding Company, September 11, 1918; F. T. Bowles to Merrill Stevens Co., October 8, 1917, File 19262-1; Jax Concrete Shipyard to Dept. Concrete Ship Construction, August 7, 1918, File 19203-1, all in Record Group 32, Emergency Fleet Corporation, National Archives; *FTU*, November 1, 25, 1917, May 31, July 1, 25, August 3, October 1, 1918; Davis, *History of Jacksonville*, 270. Included in the 63 percent increase in the cost of living

were food prices (up 60 percent), clothing (128 percent), furniture (131 percent), and fuel (28 percent).

16. *FTU*, May 24, 29, 1918; W. J. Haines to William Towers, Transportation and Housing Division, July 27, 1920, "Fletcher Park, South Jacksonville, Florida," Record Group 32, National Archives.

17. *FTU*, August 18, 25, September 15, November 14, 1917; Davis, *History of Jacksonville*, 258–59.

18. Russell Mott, Morale Officer, Camp Joseph E. Johnston, Florida, to Chief, Morale Branch, General Staff, Washington, D.C., November 29, 1918; "All Pt of 348" to Major Gen. [William P.] Duvall, December 11, 1918; Russell Mott to Chief, Morale Division, General Staff, Washington, D.C., December 13, 1918; Russell Mott to Chief, Morale Division, General Staff, Washington, D.C., December 14, 1918, all in Record Group 165, National Archives.

19. *FTU*, April 3, 6, 1918.

20. Ibid., April 4, 8, 17, July 3, 1918; City Council Minute Book, May 7, July 2, 1918.

21. *FTU*, April 15, 1918.

22. Ibid., April 21, 1918.

23. Ibid., April 24, 1918; "Minutes of the Jacksonville City Council" (Minute Book City Hall), April 23, 1918.

24. *FTU*, July 5, 1918.

25. Ibid., July 10, 16, 1918.

26. Davis, *History of Jacksonville*, 272; John Doggett to Peter Knight, June 17, 1918, File Folder 18248-1, Record Group 332, National Archives.

27. *FTU*, August 22, September 4, October 18, 1918, June 28, July 3, 1919.

28. David M. Kennedy, *Over Here: The First World War and American Society* (New York: Oxford University Press, 1980), chapter 1, esp. 68, 73.

29. Davis, *History of Jacksonville*, 273, prints MacDonnell's report on the epidemic to the city commission, dated December 21, 1920. See also *FTU* and *Metropolis* from mid-September to mid-November, 1918.

30. Davis, *History of Jacksonville*, 273; *FTU*, October 22, 25, November 3, 1918.

31. Davis, *History of Jacksonville*, 274; *Report of the City Commission of Jacksonville, Florida, Covering the Year 1917 to 1920* (Jacksonville, 1921), 157–60.

32. Alfred W. Crosby, Jr., *Epidemic and Peace, 1918* (Westport, Conn.: Greenwood Press, 1976), 86, 114.

33. Davis, *History of Jacksonville*, 257–58.

34. *FTU*, January 5, 1919; Senator Duncan U. Fletcher to Charles Piez, General Manager, Emergency Fleet Corporation, March 5, 1919, and W. J. Haines, Staff Assistant, Transportation and Housing Operations Division to William Towers, Manager, Transportation and Housing Operations, July 27, 1920, Record Group 32, of the U.S. Shipping Board, National Archives, Washington, D.C.

35. *FTU*, February 18, 26, March 2, May 29, June 5, July 1, 21, September 23, 24, October 13, December 13, 16, 1919.

36. Ibid., March 20, 24, 1919.

37. Ibid., December 17, 1918, April 16, August 3, 11, 29, September 1, 1919; City Council Minute Book, June 5, 1919.

38. Ibid., March 6, 7, 10, May 11, June 20, July 1, 19, 1919.

39. Davis, *History of Jacksonville*, 275–76.

40. Wayne Flynt, "Florida Labor Relations and Political Radicalism, 1919–1920," *Labor History* 9 (Winter 1968): 74.

41. *FTU*, June 10, 11, 12, 1919.

42. Ibid., July 2, 8, 12, 16, 17, 1919; City Council minute book, June 1, 8, 1919. Flynt's "Florida Labor Relations and Political Radicalism" is quite inaccurate on this strike.

43. Robert K. Murray, *Red Scare: A Study in National Hysteria, 1919–1920* (Minneapolis: University of Minnesota Press, 1955), esp. chap. 1; *FTU*, June 28, July 3, 1919.

44. Flynt, "Florida Labor Relations and Political Radicalism," 84.

45. *FTU*, May 5, 1919.

46. *FTU*, August 21, September 8, 9, 1919.

47. Ibid., September 9, 10, 11, 12, 16, 17, 1919.

48. *FTU*, October 14, 1919; Jerrell H. Shofner, "Florida and Black Migration," *Florida Historical Quarterly* 62, no. 3 (January 1979): 285.

49. *FTU*, May 24, 28, June 5, 8, 1919.

50. Ibid., June 11, 12, December 19, 1919.

Chapter 7

1. Assessed property values are found in the *Florida Times-Union*, January 1, 1902 (hereafter cited as *FTU*), and the *Report of the City Commission of the City of Jacksonville, Florida* (Jacksonville, 1921), 9; the number of workers engaged in manufacturing and the value of their product are listed in the U.S. Bureau of Census, *Twelfth Census of the United States, Part II*, Census Bulletin no. 101 (Washington, 1900), table 7, and Bureau of Census, *Fourteenth Census of the United States*, State Compendium, Florida (Washington, 1924), table 14. Bank deposits and clearings for both years are listed in *Report of the City Commission*, 9; imports and exports are listed in the *FTU*, January 1, 1901, and *Report of the River and Harbor Committee of the Jacksonville Chamber of Commerce to the United States Army Engineers, Jacksonville Florida* (Jacksonville, 1922), 10.

2. Dewey W. Grantham, *Southern Progressivism, the Reconciliation of Progress and Tradition* (Knoxville: University of Tennessee Press, 1983), 276–90, discusses the modernizing southern city in the context of progressivism across the region. Other studies of southern cities in the Progressive Era include George M. Reynolds, *Machine Politics in New Orleans, 1887–1926* (reprint, New York: AMS Press, 1968); John Joseph Duffy, "Charleston Politics in the Progressive Era" (Ph.D. diss., University of South Carolina, 1963); David Ernest Alsobrook, "Ala-

bama's Port City: Mobile during the Progressive Era. 1896–1917" (Ph.D. diss., Auburn University, 1983); Richard Henry Lee German, "The Queen City of the Savannah: Augusta, Georgia, during the Progressive Era, 1890–1917" (Ph.D. diss., University of Florida, 1973); Thomas Mashburn Deaton, "Atlanta during the Progressive Era" (Ph.D. diss., University of Georgia, 1969); Samuel Millard Kipp III, "Urban Growth and Social Change in the South, 1870–1920: Greensboro, North Carolina as a Case Study" (Ph.D. diss., Princeton University, 1974); William D. Miller, *Memphis during the Progressive Era, 1900–1917* (Memphis, Tenn.: Memphis State University Press, 1957); and James B. Crooks, *Politics and Progress: The Rise of Urban Progressivism in Baltimore, 1895–1911* (Baton Rouge: Louisiana State University Press, 1968); Don H. Doyle, *New Men, New Cities, New South: Atlanta, Nashville, Charleston, Mobile, 1860–1910* (Chapel Hill: University of North Carolina Press, 1990).

An interesting discussion of the development of public policy affecting a New South city can be seen in George W. Hopkins, "From Naval Pauper to Naval Power: The Development of Charleston's Metropolitan-Military Complex," in *The Martial Metropolis, U.S. Cities in War and Peace*, ed. Roger W. Lotchin (New York: Praeger, 1984), 1–34, and in James R. McGovern, "Pensacola, Florida: A Military City in the New South," *Florida Historical Quarterly* 59 (July 1980): 24–41.

3. While the emphasis of this study has been on the developmental, "progressive" character (except in race relations) of the New South Jacksonville community, I would be amiss to ignore the romantic nostalgia for the Old South and Lost Cause of the Confederacy that Paul Gaston and others have so ably described. One of the most recent additions to this genre is Gaines M. Foster, *Ghosts of the Confederacy: Defeat, the Lost Cause, and the Emergence of the New South, 1865 to 1913* (New York: Oxford University Press, 1987). Jacksonville, too, had its romantic memories, perhaps best exemplified in the twenty-fourth annual Confederate reunion held locally May 6–8, 1914, to which some 60,000 veterans went, camping in what later was renamed Confederate Park just north of downtown. The *FTU* and *The Metropolis* gave full coverage to the event. T. Frederick Davis, *History of Jacksonville, Florida and Vicinity, 1513–1924* (Jacksonville: Florida Historical Society, 1925), 247, mentions it briefly.

4. J. C. Wiggins and Co. *Jacksonville Directory, 1900*; R. L. Polk and Co. *Jacksonville City Directory, 1920* (Jacksonville: author, 1920).

5. Ibid.

6. Most of the birthplaces are listed in the biographical sections of George M. Chapin, *Florida, 1513–1913, Past and Future*, 2 vols. (Chicago, Ill.: S. J. Clarke Publishing Co., 1914), and Pleasant Daniel Gold, *History of Duval County, Florida* (St. Augustine, Fla.: The Record Co., 1928). The exceptions are Johnson, Randolph, and Jennings listed in their biographies, and Conroy listed in the *FTU*, August 22, 1920. Blodgett is listed in Clement Richardson, ed., *Cyclopedia of the*

Colored Race, (Montgomery, Ala.: National Publishing Co., 1919), 1: 435, and John Gregg is listed in R. R. Wright, ed. and comp., *Encyclopedia of African Methodism* (Philadelphia: author, 1947), 122.

7. James Weldon Johnson, *Along This Way* (reprint; New York: De Capo Press, 1973), 299.

8. The riot after the Johnson fight is described in the *FTU*, July 5, 6, 16, 1910. The appeal about the shooting of thirty blacks is in the "Minutes of Board of Governors Meetings of Jacksonville Board of Trade," December 15, 1914, on deposit at the Jacksonville Chamber of Commerce.

9. Joel Williamson, *The Crucible of Race: Black-White Relations* in *The American South Since Emancipation* (New York: Oxford University Press, 1984), esp. chaps. 4 and 9. For a look at the views of southern intellectuals about race during this era, see Bruce Clayton, *The Savage Ideal: Intolerance and Intellectual Leadership in the South, 1890–1914* (Baltimore, Md.: Johns Hopkins University Press, 1972), esp. chap. 8.

10. I. A. Newby, *Plain Folk in the New South: Social Change and Cultural Persistence, 1880–1915* (Baton Rouge: Louisiana State University Press, 1989), 491.

11. The 1920 census reported 41,520 blacks (45 percent), 49,972 whites (55 percent), and 66 Asians.

12. Robert P. Ingalls, *Urban Vigilantes in the New South: Tampa, 1882–1936* (Knoxville: University of Tennessee Press, 1988), portrays the violence in Florida's second city. For Bowden's actions, see *FTU*, August 1, 1915.

13. Philip Warren Miller, "Greater Jacksonville's Response to the Florida Land Boom of the 1920s" (Master's thesis, University of Florida, 1989), chap. 1; George Strayer, dir., *Report of the Survey of the Schools of Duval County, Florida* (New York: Teachers College, Columbia University, 1927).

14. Miller, "Greater Jacksonville's Response to the Florida Land Boom."

15. *FTU*, October 25, 1913; Robert S. McElvaine, *The Great Depression: America, 1929–1941* (New York: Times Books, 1984), esp. chap. 9.

16. Woman's Club of Jacksonville, *Annual Report, 1912–1913* (Jacksonville, 1913), 38.

NOTE ON SOURCES

In this section I do not attempt to list all the sources on Jacksonville history. Rather I intend to note materials of particular significance to this study, and, thereby, serve as a guide for scholars and other readers.

Manuscripts

In an earlier book about Baltimore, Maryland, I wrote that the "biggest problem confronting the historian of the city is the paucity of private papers remaining from earlier times." This condition continues to exist. Civic leaders met frequently in person and communicated by telephone. Rarely did they keep whatever correspondence they did write or receive. As a result, manuscript materials are relatively unimportant to this study, with some exceptions.

The May Mann Jennings letters on deposit at the P. K. Yonge Library, University of Florida, provided useful information about her work with the Woman's Club of Jacksonville. The T. Frederick Davis Collection, Claude L'Engle Papers, Napoleon Broward Papers, Otis L. Keene diaries, and Edwin Hansford Rennolds diaries were marginally helpful.

A second useful collection came from the National Archives, where correspondence from Senator Duncan Fletcher and others on issues related to establishing municipal docks and the Acosta Bridge (Office of Chief of Engineers Document File, Record Group 77), Camp Sidney Johnston (Office of the Adjutant General Document File, Record Group 94, and War Department Record Group 165), and Fletcher Park (United States Shipping Board Emergency Fleet Corporation, Record Group 32) were quite helpful.

Disappointing were the governors' papers in the Florida State Library for Williams S. Jennings (1901–5), Napoleon B. Broward (1905–9), Albert W. Gilchrist (1909–13), Parke Trammell (1913–17), and Sidney J. Catts (1917–21).

For African-American history, the Eartha M. M. White Collection at the University of North Florida helped, as did Louis R. Harlan et al., eds., *The Booker T. Washington Papers* (Urbana: University of Illinois Press, 1976–83). The James Weldon Johnson Papers at Yale University had little material relating to his Jacksonville years.

Another form of manuscript is the minute book. The Minutes of Jacksonville City Council from 1901 to 1920 on file at the City Council were useful, as were the Minutes of the Duval County School Board for the same years on deposit at the school board. The Minutes of the Jacksonville Chamber of Commerce for 1914–20 supplemented the annual reports of that organization.

Of major importance for sampling and classifying Jacksonville's work force were the U.S. Census manuscripts on microfilm for 1900 and 1910.

Documents

Available documents were public and private, federal, state, and local. Among the public documents, the U.S. Bureau of the Census, *Twelfth Census of the United States, Part II, Statistics of Population* (Washington, D.C.: Bureau of the Census, 1900) plus its Census Bulletins, nos. 16, 72, and 75; *Thirteenth Census of the United States Taken in the Year 1910*, vol. 1. *Population* (Washington, D.C.: Government Printing Office, 1913); and *Fourteenth Census of the United States, State Compendium, Florida* (Washington, D.C.: Government Printing Office, 1924), provided basic population data. The Bureau of Census, *Statistics of Cities Having a Population of Over 30,000, 1908* (Washington, D.C.: Government Printing Office, 1910), was useful. Also helpful was the annual *Report of the Chief of Engineers, U.S. Army* (Washington, D.C.: Government Printing Office) with regard to the development of the St. Johns River.

On the state level, the Florida Department of Agriculture published *Population of Florida Taken in 1905* (Tallahassee, 1905) and *Fourth Census of the State of Florida Taken in the Year 1915* (Tallahassee, 1915). For education, *Biennial Reports of the Superintendent of Public Instruction for the State of Florida* (Tallahassee, Fla., 1900–1920), proved useful, as were the *Annual Reports of the State Board of Health of Florida* and the *Annual Report of the Railroad Commission of the State of Florida* (Jacksonville: The Commission).

On the local level, the City of Jacksonville published an *Annual Report of the Board of Health*, beginning in 1910. The Board of Bond Trustees for the Waterworks and Improvement Bonds of the City of Jacksonville (popularly known as the Board of Bond Trustees), also published an annual report through the entire era, as did the Board of Trustees for the Public Library. Following the creation of the city commission, the *Report of the City Commission of the City of Jacksonville, Florida* from the years 1917 to 1920 (Jacksonville, 1921) proved useful.

In the private sector, the Jacksonville Board of Trade *Reports*, published annually through 1914, and the Woman's Club of Jacksonville, *Annual Report*, from 1906 to 1920, were important. So, too, were Charles H. Smith, *Report of the Jacksonville Relief Association* (Jacksonville, 1901); the *First Annual Report of the Associated Charities, Jacksonville, Florida, March 16–December 31, 1910* (Jacksonville, 1911); Seaboard Air Line Railway, *Mercantile and Industrial Review of Jacksonville, Florida* (Portsmouth, Va., 1906); and Jacksonville Chamber of Commerce, *Industrial Survey of Jacksonville, Florida* (Jacksonville, 1915).

Other contemporary descriptions of Jacksonville include Sidney Lanier, *Florida: Its Scenery, Climate and History* (1875; reprint, Gainesville: University of Florida Press, 1973), James Esgate, *Jacksonville: The Metropolis of Florida* (Boston: W. G. M. Perry, 1885), S. Paul Brown, *The Book of Jacksonville; A History* (Poughkeepsie, N.Y.: A. V. Haight, printer, 1893), Benjamin Harrison, *Acres of Ashes* (Jacksonville, Fla.: J. A. Holloman, 1901), Charles H. Smith, *Jacksonville and Florida Facts* (Jacksonville, Fla.: H. and W. B. Drew Co., 1906), R. T. Arnold, *Jacksonville, 'Aziz'* (Jacksonville, Fla. Jacksonville Chamber of Commerce, 1920).

Newspapers and Periodicals

Probably the greatest source for urban history is the daily newspaper, though it must be read with concern for what is omitted as well as for what it says. *The Florida Times-Union* was Jacksonville's daily morning and Sunday newspaper with circulation across the state. It was readily accessible on microfilm at several locations. *The Metropolis* was an afternoon daily available on microfilm beginning with 1907. Though several black weekly newspapers were published during the era, none survive. The same essentially applies to *The Artisan*, a labor paper, and to Claude L'Engle's weekly *Sun*, though I saw one copy of *The Artisan* in the National Archives and a few copies of the *Sun* in the L'Engle Papers at the University of Florida.

Another major periodical source was the Jacksonville city directories, beginning with J. Wiggins and Co., *Jacksonville City Directory, 1900* (Jacksonville, Fla.: Author, 1900). In 1902 R. L. Polk and Company assumed publication and continued therein throughout the era.

Memoirs, Autobiographies, and Reminiscences

A very important autobiography for portraying the changing racial attitudes of the era was James Weldon Johnson, *Along This Way* (New York: Viking Press, 1933), republished by De Capo Press in 1973. Less useful was Bion H. Barnett, *Reminiscences of Fifty Years in the Barnett Bank* (Jacksonville, Fla., 1927).

Biographies

The best biographies for Jacksonville in this era were Wayne Flynt's two books, *Duncan Upshaw Fletcher; Dixie's Reluctant Progressive* (Tallahassee: Florida State University Press, 1971), and *Cracker Messiah: Governor Sidney J. Catts of Florida* (Baton Rouge: Louisiana State University Press, 1977). Also useful for the African-American experience were Jervis Anderson, *A. Philip Randolph, A Biographical Portrait* (New York: Harcourt Brace Jovanovich, 1972); and Eugene Levy, *James Weldon Johnson: Black Leader, Black Voice* (Chicago: University of Chicago Press, 1973). Linda D. Vance, *May Mann Jennings, Florida's Genteel Activist* (Gainesville: University of Florida Press, 1985), offered important insights on women's experiences. I also consulted Samuel Proctor, *Napoleon Bonaparte Broward: Florida's Fighting Democrat* (Gainesville: University of Florida Press,

1950); Lillian Gilkes, *Cora Crane, A Biography of Mrs. Stephen Crane* (Bloomington: Indiana University Press, 1960); Richard A. Martin, *The City Makers* (Jacksonville, Fla.: Convention Press, 1972); Robert C. Broward, *The Architecture of Henry John Klutho: The Prairie School in Jacksonville* (Jacksonville: University of North Florida Press, 1983); and Edward N. Akin, *Flagler, Rockefeller Partner & Florida Pioneer* (Kent, Oh.: Kent State University Press, 1988).

Monographs, Articles, and Other Works

Regarding general histories of Jacksonville, T. Frederick Davis, *History of Jacksonville, Florida and Vicinity, 1513 to 1924* (Jacksonville: Florida Historical Society, 1925), is the first book one turns to, but it is severely dated and virtually omits any reference to one-half of Jacksonville's population during this era. James Robertson Ward, *Old Hickory's Town: An Illustrated History of Jacksonville* (Jacksonville: Florida Publishing Co., 1982), has a little more than one chapter devoted to this era. Wayne W. Wood, *Jacksonville's Architectural Heritage: Landmarks for the Future* (Jacksonville: University of North Florida Press, 1989), is an encyclopedia of information about the physical remains from the city in this time period. Pleasant Daniel Gold, *History of Duval County, Florida* (St. Augustine, Fla.: The Record Company, 1928), is most useful for its biographical sketches of contemporaries.

Other books and monographs that touch on the Jacksonville scene in this era included Edward C. Williams, *Florida Politics in the Gilded Age, 1877–1893* (Gainesville: University of Florida Press, 1973); David R. Colburn and Richard K. Scher, *Florida's Gubernatorial Politics in the Twentieth Century* (Tallahassee: Florida State University Press, 1980); Peter D. Klingman, *Neither Dies Nor Surrenders: A History of the Republican Party in Florida, 1867–1970* (Gainesville: University of Florida Press, 1984); William T. Cash, *History of the Democratic Party in Florida* (Tallahassee: Florida Democratic Historical Foundation, 1936); Barbara Ann Richardson, *A History of Blacks in Jacksonville, Florida, 1860–1895: A Socioeconomic and Political Study* (Ann Arbor, Mich.: University Microfilms, 1975); Richard Alan Nelson, *Florida and the American Motion Picture Industry, 1898–1980* (New York: Garland Publishing, 1983); and J. Irving E. Scott, *The Education of Black People in Florida* (Philadelphia, Pa.: Dorrance, 1974). Of marginal value were George E. Buker, *Sun, Sand and Water: A History of the Jacksonville District U.S. Army Corps of Engineers* (Jacksonville, Fla.: G. E. Buker, 1975); Natalie H. Glickstein, *That Ye May Remember: Congregation Ahavath Chesed, 1882–1982, 5642–5742* (St. Petersburg, Fla.: Byron Kennedy, 1982); Richard A. Martin, *St. Luke's Hospital, A Century of Service, 1873–1973* (Jacksonville, Fla.: n.p., 1973); Dena Snodgrass, *The Island of Ortega, A History* (Jacksonville, Fla.: Ortega School, 1981); and George Hallam, *Riverside Remembered* (Jacksonville, Fla.: Drummond Press, 1976).

Three recent master's theses that add to the era are Kathleen Ann Francis Cohen, "Immigrant Jacksonville: A Profile of Immigrant Groups in Jacksonville, Florida, 1890–1920" (University of Florida, 1986), Linda Emerson Sabin, "Nursing and Health Care in Jacksonville, Florida, 1900–1930" (University of Florida,

1988), and Philip Warren Miller, "Greater Jacksonville's Response to the Florida Land Boom of the 1920s" (University of Florida, 1989). Of less value is Emily Howard Atkins, "A History of Jacksonville, Florida, 1816–1902" (Duke University, 1941).

Useful journal articles included Edward N. Akin, "Where a Minority Becomes a Majority: Blacks in Jacksonville Politics," *Florida Historical Quarterly* 53 (October 1974) 123–145; August Meier and Elliot Rudwick, "The Boycott Movement Against Jim Crow Streetcars in the South, 1900–1906," *Journal of American History* 55 (March 1969): 756–75; James B. Crooks, "Changing Face of Jacksonville, Florida: 1900–1914," *Florida Historical Quarterly* 62 (April 1984): 439–63; James B. Crooks, "Jacksonville in the Progressive Era: Responses to Urban Growth," *Florida Historical Quarterly* 65 (July 1986): 52–71; James B. Crooks, "Leisure Time in Jacksonville: 1900 to World War I," *Journal of Regional Culture* 4 (Spring/Summer 1984): 61–68; David T. Courtwright, "The Hidden Epidemic: Opiate Addiction and Cocaine Use in the South, 1860–1920," *Journal of Southern History* 49 (February 1983): 57–72; David T. Courtwright, "Charles Terry, *The Opium Problem*, and American Narcotic Policy," *Journal of Drug Issues* 16 (1983): 421–34; Emily Howard Atkins, "The 1913 Campaign for Child Labor in Florida," *Florida Historical Quarterly* 35 (January 1957): 223–40; Jerrell H. Shofner, "Florida and the Black Migration," *Florida Historical Quarterly* 57 (January 1979): 267–88; Wayne Flynt, "Florida Labor and Political Radicalism, 1919–1920," *Labor History* 9 (Winter 1968): 73–90; Kenneth R. Johnson, "Florida Women Get the Vote," *Florida Historical Quarterly* 48 (January 1970): 299–312; Joel Webb Eastman, "Claude L'Engle, Florida Muckraker," *Florida Historical Quarterly* 45 (January 1967): 243–52; and A. Elizabeth Taylor, "The Woman Suffrage Movement in Florida," *Florida Historical Quarterly* 36 (July 1957).

Other sources of value included Clement Richardson, ed., *The National Cyclopedia of the Colored Race*, vol. 1 (Montgomery, Ala.: National Publishing Co., 1919); Daniel L. Schafer, "Eartha M. M. White: The Early Years of a Jacksonville Humanitarian" (Typescript in possession of the author, 1976); "History of the Ebeneezer United Methodist Church, Jacksonville, Florida" (Typescript, 1987); "110th Anniversary Celebration, Mt. Zion A.M.E. Church, Jacksonville, Florida" (Jacksonville, 1976); "A Brief History of the Afro-American Life Insurance Company" (Typescript, 1971); "Bethel Baptist Marks 150 Years as First Jacksonville Church," *Florida Times-Union*, October 15, 1988; and Edith Gray, "The History of the Jacksonville Red Cross, 1914–1920" (Typescript at Haydon Burns Library, n.d.).

The major conceptual framework of this book places the early twentieth-century history of Jacksonville in the context of the developing New South myth. The most thorough exposition of this myth comes from Paul Gaston, *The New South Creed: A Study in Southern Mythmaking* (New York: Knopf, 1970). Significant earlier contributions to this concept derive from C. Vann Woodward, *Origins of the New South, 1788–1913* (Baton Rouge: Louisiana State University Press, 1951), and George Brown Tindall, *The Emergence of the New South, 1913–1945* (Baton Rouge: Louisiana State University Press, 1967). Also relevant is Richard D. Brown, *Modernization: The Transformation of American Life, 1600–1865* (New York: Hill and Wang, 1976). More recently, a series of books and articles have reexamined the concept: Gavin Wright, *Old South, New South: Revolutions in the Southern Economy Since the Civil War* (New York: Basic Books, 1986); Peter Wallenstein, *From Slave South to New South: Public Policy in Nineteenth-Century Georgia* (Chapel Hill: University of North Carolina Press, 1987); Walter J. Fraser, Jr., and Winfred B. Moore, Jr., eds. *From the Old South to the New: Essays on the Transitional South* (Westport, Conn.: Greenwood Press, 1981); Orville Vernon Burton and Robert C. McMath, Jr., eds., *Toward a New South? Studies in Post–Civil War Southern Communities* (Westport, Conn.: Greenwood Press, 1982); Winfred B. Moore, Jr., et al., eds., *Developing Dixie: Modernization in a Traditional Society* (Westport, Conn.: Greenwood Press, 1988); and most recently, Don H. Doyle, *New Men, New Cities, New South: Atlanta, Nashville, Charleston, Mobile, 1860–1910* (Chapel Hill: University of North Carolina Press, 1990). Books on individual cities seen in this context include James Michael Russell, *Atlanta, 1847–1890* (Baton Rouge: Louisiana State University Press, 1988); Don H. Doyle, *Nashville in the New South, 1880–1930* (Knoxville: University of Tennessee Press, 1985); Robert P. Ingalls, *Urban Vigilantes in the New South: Tampa, 1882–1936* (Knoxville: University of Tennessee Press, 1988); and Harold L. Platt, *City Building in the New South: The Growth of Public Services in Houston, Texas, 1830–1910* (Philadelphia, Pa.: Temple University Press, 1983). To a lesser extent, Carl V. Harris, *Political Power in Birmingham, 1871–1921* (Knoxville: University of Tennessee Press, 1977), and James R. McGovern, *The Emergence of a City in the Modern South: Pensacola, 1900–1945* (Pensacola, Fla.: Painter, 1976), fit into this framework.

All studies of southern cities must be put into the context of Blaine A. Brownell and David R. Goldfield, eds., *The City in Southern History: The Growth of Urban Civilization in the South* (Port Washington, N.Y.: Kennikat Press, 1977), particularly David R. Goldfield, *Cotton Fields and Skyscrapers: Southern City and Region, 1607–1980* (Baton Rouge: Louisiana State University Press, 1982). One must also see this volume in the context of Dewey W. Grantham, *Southern Progressivism: The Reconciliation of Progress and Tradition* (Knoxville: University of Tennessee Press, 1983).

Finally, individual chapters frequently rest on concepts that I found applicable to them, from authors including Gaston in chapter 1, Stephan Thernstrom, *The Other Bostonians: Poverty and Progress in the American Metropolis, 1880–1970* (Cambridge, Mass.: Harvard University Press, 1973), in chapter 2; Gunther Barth, *City People: The Rise of Modern City Culture in Nineteenth Century America* (New York: Oxford University Press, 1980), and Ted Ownby, "Evangelicalism and Male Culture: Recreation in the Rural South, 1865–1920" (Ph.D. diss., Johns Hopkins University, 1986), for chapter 5; and Joel Williamson, *The Crucible of Race: Black-*

White Relations in the American South since Emancipation (New York: Oxford University Press, 1984), and I. A. Newby, *Plain Folk in the New South: Social Change and Cultural Persistence, 1880–1915* (Baton Rouge: Louisiana State University Press, 1989), in chapter 7. I alone am responsible, however, for whatever interpretations I have made with regard to their works.

INDEX